The Effigy Mound Culture
of Wisconsin

Doctoral Dissertation, Department of Anthropology,
University of Chicago

by
CHANDLER W. ROWE
Department of Anthropology
Lawrence College
Appleton, Wisconsin

GREENWOOD PRESS, PUBLISHERS
WESTPORT, CONNECTICUT

Originally published in 1956
by order of the Board of Trustees,
Milwaukee Public Museum, Milwaukee, Wisconsin

Reprinted with the permission
of the Milwaukee Public Museum

First Greenwood Reprinting 1970

Library of Congress Catalogue Card Number 78-111396

SBN 8371-4630-5

Printed in the United States of America

MILWAUKEE PUBLIC MUSEUM
PUBLICATIONS IN ANTHROPOLOGY

NUMBER 3

The Effigy Mound Culture
of Wisconsin

Doctoral Dissertation, Department of Anthropology,
University of Chicago

by
CHANDLER W. ROWE
Department of Anthropology
Lawrence College
Appleton, Wisconsin

ACKNOWLEDGMENTS

The writer would like to acknowledge with gratitude the kindness of W. C. McKern, Director of the Milwaukee Public Museum, for making material from the collections of the Museum available for study, for permission to use hitherto unpublished data, for supplying the necessary photographs, and for many valuable suggestions; of Robert E. Ritzenthaler, Curator of Anthropology, Milwaukee Public Museum, for cooperation in providing study materials and constructive criticism of the text; of my colleague Howard W. Troyer, Department of English, Lawrence College, for suggestions on the style of the manuscript; and of my wife, Margaret Grubbs Rowe, for, among other things, her services in proofreading.

                                        Chandler W. Rowe

Lawrence College
Appleton, Wisconsin
August, 1951

The Effigy Mound Culture of Wisconsin

TABLE OF CONTENTS

LIST OF TABLES

LIST OF ILLUSTRATIONS

Chapter I

INTRODUCTION

The archaeological assemblage that has been termed the Effigy Mound culture has been imperfectly known for some time, and varying and conflicting statements have been made concerning its origin, antiquity, and cultural affiliations. This culture has been placed in various chronological positions on numerous archaeological charts, conclusions have been drawn regarding affinities with other archaeological manifestations both in the Wisconsin province and outside, and its origin has been attributed to certain historically known groups. Yet nowhere is there a compilation of all the known data concerning the Wisconsin Effigy Mound culture. Much of the available data are not completely accurate, or at least such accuracy as they have cannot be readily ascertained. There has been a tendency for certain ideas concerning Effigy Mound to become almost traditional even though they can be demonstrated to be groundless or at best based upon insufficient evidence. It would seem that the time is at hand for reexamination of data, for new syntheses, and for possible establishment of concrete conclusions. Certainly such a study is needed before further work with Effigy Mound can be carried on. The present study has been undertaken with these thoughts in mind. Reexamination will pull together hitherto chaotic data and help to prevent the somewhat loose usage of these data that has been characteristic in the past. This study proposes to make a synthesis on the basis of published data, with additional material from certain hitherto unpublished sites. An attempt will be made to ascertain the facts relative to this culture in order to determine whether or not earlier assumptions with regard to it are valid.

No reference to the mounds appears in the reports of the early explorers through this territory. Samuel F. Haven (p. 129) has observed:

"The great horizontal dimensions of these effigies, raised but a few feet above the surface of the ground, was doubtless the reason why they failed to arrest the attention of travellers at an early period, their forms not always perceptible from a single point of view, and sometimes only developed by the measurements of the surveyor."

Haven attributes their identification to Dr. I. A. Lapham of whom he says:

"It has been remarked that the effigy mounds were first observed by Mr. Lapham, in 1836. In 1850, that gentleman entered into an arrangement with the American Antiquarian Society, and, on behalf of that institution, commenced a thorough archaeological survey of the State. His notes and drawings when completed, were transferred to the Smithsonian Institution, and constitute a portion of the volume of Contributions published in 1855."

Haven (p. 126) goes on to say:

"The region between Lake Michigan and Mississippi, now constituting the State of Wisconsin, had hitherto been comparatively unexplored for archaeological purposes; although known to present some peculiar features, and to possess remains of a singular and distinctive character.

"Works intended for defense, and such as are apparently designed for religious or sacrificial ceremonials, are there seldom found; but structures of no great elevation, though often on a scale of considerable horizontal extent, representing a variety of fanciful forms, are frequent along the courses of the streams, and by the borders of the lakes.

"The figures are described as chiefly those of Lizards, Turtles, Birds, Bears, Foxes and men; combined with straight lines, angles, crosses, curves and other simple embankments."

Squier and Davis (pp. 124-5) report that "The first public notice of these relics . . . was made by Richard C. Taylor, Esq. in the 'American Journal of Science and Art,' for the month of April 1838. A later motive by Prof. John Locke constituted a short chapter in the 'Report on the Mineral Lands of the United States' . . . published in 1844."

One of the most interesting circumstances regarding the Effigy Mound culture is its distribution within a very limited and compact area. Extensive mound exploration on the part of Cyrus Thomas (1890, p. 531) led him to say that the effigy mound area ". . . may be designated by the following boundary line: Starting on the shore of Lake Michigan a little south of the line between Wisconsin and Illinois, it runs westward to the vicinity of the Rock River, where it makes a sudden curve southward to include an extension down the valley of that river a short distance into Illinois. Bending northwest, it strikes the Mississippi very near the extreme southwest corner of Wisconsin. Passing a short distance westward into Iowa, it bends northward, including about two counties in this state and the extreme southeastern county of Minnesota. Thence, recrossing the Mississippi a little north of Lacrosse, it continues in a nearly direct line to the head of Green Bay; thence south along the shore of Lake Michigan to the starting point. It is possible the boundary will be extended farther northward when that portion of the state has been more thoroughly explored. Nevertheless, the indications are that comparatively few effigies will be found outside the line given; in fact, when we pass north of the Fox river on the eastern slope, and the latitude of Adams county in the Wisconsin valley, works of this class are rare."

Exploration during the years following Thomas' report has not changed to any great extent the limits of the area which he defined. It is apparent from the above description that the mounds under consideration here are confined almost entirely to a broad band which covers the southern portion of Wisconsin (Fig. 1). The number of mounds in Illinois, Iowa, and Minnesota are few, whereas those of Wisconsin may be counted in the thousands.

That the Effigy Mound culture is concentrated in Wisconsin is brought home by the fact that the only available published data which report excavations and analysis of the sites of this culture are the work of the archaeologists of the

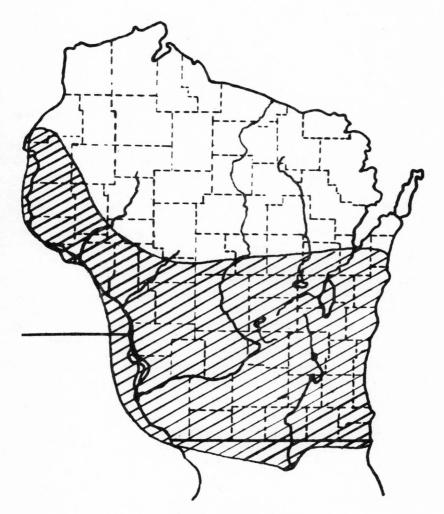

Fig. 1. Map of Effigy Mound Distribution.

Milwaukee Public Museum. So far as the writer can determine, no reports of this nature have been forthcoming from the marginal areas of Illinois, Iowa, or Minnesota.

It is somewhat unusual, therefore, that so little information is available concerning these works of aboriginal settlers. Undoubtedly many of them were dug by relic hunters, and the artifacts obtained never made known. The fact that these mounds rarely yield an abundance of objects representing material culture may have a bearing on the present state of knowledge. A large amount of dirt must be moved for the little information obtained. Braidwood (pp. 110-11) elaborates on what he has termed the "human element" involved in the completeness of the archaeological record, and several of his statements will bear repeating:

"Two types of human element are involved as regards the completeness of the archaeological record. The first of these implies that some one ancient people may have been (unwittingly) more considerate of the archaeologist than was his neighbor. Thus certain habits in the normal culture pattern . . . leaves us more materials from some peoples than others. Or, we may find much material, but of a sort which reflects some one specialized kind of activity. The 'human element' in the archaeologist himself, finally, is often to blame for gaps in the record."

Here he is pointing out that the archaeologist may interest himself in particular problems to the exclusion of others. As a rule, it is true, more cultural prehistory can be written when it is based upon the excavation of archaeological sites which are rich in material remains. However, the chronology is incomplete unless time is also taken to unearth the remains of those cultures carried by groups which may appear to have been poverty stricken by comparison. The people responsible for the manifestation which we call the Effigy Mound culture have a place in the cultural history of the Wisconsin province and, although all of the facts are not in, a synthesis of the data at hand should help to make that sequence a little more clear.

Since the earliest discovery of the effigy mounds, speculation as to their purpose has run high. Many of the various speculations are based on little actual excavation, with a resulting number of contradictions. We read such statements as those of Thomas (1890, p. 531): "The comparatively few excavations which have been made in these works indicate that they were not intended for burial purposes, nor has anything yet been observed which would lead to the belief that they were thrown up for dwelling sites."

In the words of Louis Folge, M.D. (p. 141), "Old settlers state that in the early 50's this region Rockland Township was overrun by roaming bands of Pottawatomies. These Indians explained the presence of these mounds by stating that there 'had been a big battle' here and that these were the burial places of the slain, a common misconception of the purposes of such earthworks."

Haven (p. 129) remarks, "The emblematic tumuli were seldom seen in isolated positions, but usually in groups, with a mound at some elevated point, commanding a view of the whole. They yielded no relics to illustrate the habits and arts of their builders, or the design of construction."

Incidentally, Haven (128-9) had a rather original idea concerning the purpose of the mounds.

"Wisconsin's aboriginal monuments are anomalous and strange, appearing not so much like structures for any sacred or civil purposes as like hieroglyphic or symbolic characters. If instead of being clustered on the surface of the earth they had been drawn on rocks and stones, efforts would be made to read them as records. They would derive a superior interest from the supposition that they are, as has been suggested, the 'totems' of tribes, perhaps memorials of amity or alliance, written upon the ground where adverse nations were accustomed to meet in peace. It must be confessed that pictorial writing on so immense a scale, with a sovereign state for a tablet, is a phenomenon uparalleled in monumental history."

Yet at the time these various statements were made Lapham (p. 9) and Hoy had completed some excavations and had published the remark:

"We excavated fourteen of the mounds, some with the greatest care; they were all sepulcharal, of a uniform construction . . . . Most of them contained more than one skeleton . . . . We could detect no stratification, each mound having been built at one time, and not by successive additions. It is quite common to find skeletons before reaching the primitive receptacle or pit. These were undoubtedly subsequent interments, made by the modern Indians."

Much of the speculation and difference of opinion can be understood by the fact that archaeological technique has become sharpened and developed to a great extent since those times. Present methods, when properly used, enable the excavator to obtain more control over the data as it is recovered, with the result that more data of an accurate and dependable nature can be obtained. With regard to a skull which he recovered from a conical mound, Lapham (p. 9) tells us, "To give the reader more particular information respecting the supposed characteristics of this interesting relic of an extinct people, I have, with the assistance of a *phrenologist friend* (italics mine), prepared the following chart." The chart presents a long list indicating the degree to which certain personality characteristics are present in the skull. He (Lapham, pp. 81-82) then concludes, "Whether these figures can be relied upon as indicating the character and disposition of the individual to whom the skull belonged, may be doubted; though it will be perceived that their indications correspond with the general character of the aborigines in the large cautiousness, individuality, etc., and the deficient constructiveness, calculations, etc." Use of such methods, if it was ever wide spread, is, of course, no longer current. The same is true of the methods of excavation. We know now, as evidence presented later in this paper will indicate, that the mounds were actually used primarily for burial purposes. The suggestion of totem affiliations is also dealt with in following pages.

Certain terms used in this paper need definition. The term *Effigy Mound culture* as it is used here includes not only the culture responsible for the effigy mound, which is its primary identifying feature, but also for the low-domed conical and linear mounds which generally occur abundantly on these sites. The material encountered in all these mounds is so similar that both the effigy mounds and accompanying types are regarded as products of the Effigy Mound culture.

The most common feature found in the mounds is the so-called *altar*. Its use in the terminology here is merely a continuation of that established by McKern (1928, p. 263), who says:

"The use of any sort of fireplace inclusively present in one of these mounds, in a majority of instances associated as they are with inclusive burials, and in one instance containing charred, human teeth, could hardly have been other than ceremonial. Whether or not they can be truly designated as altars is a matter wholly dependent upon definition. Similar features have long been called altars in this and neighboring provinces, and I can see no objection to such terminology so long as its applied use is clearly defined. The tendency on the part of some students of archeology to become hysterical over the application of the term 'altar' to features found in middle western mounds . . . seems altogether petty and little short of ridiculous. The word altar . . . has been arbitrarily selected to distinguish a stone fireplace found inclusively situated in a mound whose character, according to all available evidence, is that of a burial place, from a fireplace found occurring outside a mound and in an environment suggestive of practical, domestic use, rather than ceremonial use."

In this report, the term is expanded to include both stone and earthen fireplaces found in the mounds.

The term *cist* has also been in use for some time. It is defined (McKern, 1928, p. 263) as ". . . a small bowl-shaped type of structure with more or less vertical walls of red, unbaked clay, reinforced to some extent with pebbles, and with a slightly concave bottom lined with stones."

The present study of the Effigy Mound culture is based upon 482 mounds of various types found at thirteen known sites, eleven of which have been published. One of the unpublished ones is included in this report, and another, the Heller Group, excavated by the author, is in preparation. The following table (Table 1) shows the breakdown by type (the type terminology will be discussed later in the paper).

Table 1 indicates that the sample in some cases is smaller than would be desirable. This is due partly to the fact that some types are more numerous than others, and partly to the preference of the investigators in selecting the types to be excavated.

TABLE 1

TABULATION OF MOUNDS BY TYPE AND NUMBER EXCAVATED

Mound Type	Total Number	Number Excavated
Conical	267	82
Oval	17	8
Biconical	6	6
Linear	40	14
Panther	34	24
Bear	20	9
Bird	24	10
Deer	11	8
Buffalo	1	1
Turtle	4	2
Beaver	1	1
Canine	16	3
Problematical	42	25
Total	483	193

The distribution of the mound types by site is as follows:

Utley Mound Group

Panther 4
Bear 2
Linear 1

Green Lake Site

Oval 1

Neale Mound Group

Conical 47
Bear 15
Panther 6
Bird 3
Beaver 1
Problematical 16

McClaughry Group I

Conical 43
Biconical 5
Oval 4
Linear 3
Panther 1
Bear 1
Bird 1
Problematical 2

McClaughry Group II

Conical 22

Raisbeck Mound Group

Conical 38
Linear 14
Bird 13
Canine 11
Oval 3
Problematical 1

Kletzien Mound Group

Deer 7
Panther 6
Linear 5
Conical 4
Oval 2
Problematical 9

Kratz Creek Mound Group

Conical 31
Panther 6
Linear 2
Bear 2
Bird 1
Deer 1
Turtle 1
Problematical 6

Ross Mound Group

Conical 27
Oval 1
Biconical 1
Linear 1
Problematical 1

Diamond Bluff Mound Group

Conical 35
Linear 4
Oval 3
Panther 1

Heller Mound Group

Panther 5
Problematical 1

This study will present the raw material from the unpublished Raisbeck Mound Group; a general consideration of the Effigy Mound culture as a whole derived from all the known data, both published and unpublished; a discussion of the possible cultural relationships inside as well as outside of the area; and an inquiry into such questions as the possible connection of the Effigy Mound culture with historic groups known to have inhabited the same general region. Many of the problems which arise cannot be answered by means of the data now at hand. It is to be hoped that this study will be useful to interested archaeologists, and that it will stimulate sufficient research to bring to light additional information leading to the solution of some of the problems which cannot be answered here.

Chapter II

THE RAISBECK MOUND GROUP

The Raisbeck Mound Group is located in Grant County, Wisconsin, in Township 3 North, Range 4 West, Section 5, Western half, on the property of Mr. Clarence Raisbeck (1932). It is made up of eighty mounds, including thirty-eight conicals, fourteen linears, thirteen bird mounds, eleven canines, three ovals, and one problematical form (Fig. 2a).

The mound group and the materials found during excavation in 1932, by a Milwaukee Public Museum field party, directed by W. C. McKern, have never been published. All of the records for the Raisbeck site are not complete because of the fact that time and funds were running out at the end of the season. However, they are sufficiently comprehensible to permit much valuable data to be gathered from them. Since this group can be considered typical of many Effigy Mound culture sites, it is briefly described here for two reasons: first, in order to make the data known; and second, to present it as a typical site of the culture under consideration, as an indication of the kind of material used to draw the more general and comprehensive view of the Effigy Mound culture which is presented in later pages.

Not all of the known effigy types are to be found at the Raisbeck site; in fact only five types are recognized. However, this is true of all mound groups of the Effigy Mound culture. The writer does not know of a single site which includes one mound of each of the known types or shapes. Many of the groups located throughout the State are not as large as the Raisbeck Group. For example, the Utley Group is composed of four panthers, two bears, and one linear (McKern, 1928, p. 228). As a matter of fact, the mound group described here is the second largest in the state, as reported by reliable sources; the largest being the Neale Group, reported by McKern (1928).

DESCRIPTION OF THE MOUNDS

Mound 1 (Fig. 3a)

A conical mound with a diameter of 26 feet and approximately 4 feet in maximum height. The mound was constructed of light, chalky soil mottled with reddish and brownish elements which rested on dull reddish clay. No humus line was apparent nor was the mound stratified.

One inclusive bundle reburial was encountered in the center of the mound above the floor (Fig. 2b). This burial represented the remains of four individuals. One was an adult male whose skull exhibited no cradle-board deformation. The bones of the other individuals were in a poor state of preservation and no data could be obtained from them.

Fig. 2. a. The Raisbeck Site; b. Burial, Mound 1 (MPM Negs. 408292, 408271).

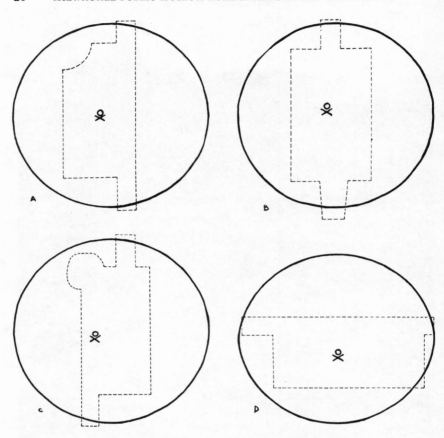

Fig. 3.   Raisbeck Group: a. Mound 1; b. Mound 2; c. Mound 3; d. Mound 4.

Four altars were encountered, all located a few inches above the mound floor. Two of the three stone altars were found 9 and 10 feet south of the center of the mound, respectively, while the third was situated 3 feet northwest from the mound center. All were composed of sandstone which was pink in color due to exposure to fire. Associated with Altar 3 was a cluster of grit-tempered, cord-impressed rim sherds apparently belonging to a single pot. The fourth altar consisted of an area approximately 4.5 feet in diameter, indicated by the presence of burned red and brown clay and charcoal. This earthen altar was situated 0.5 feet above the floor and 2.5 feet east of the center of the mound.

Mound 2 (Fig. 3b)

This conical had a diameter of 25 feet and a maximum height of 2.5 feet. It was similar to Mound 1 in the character of the soil and in that it exhibited neither stratification nor a definite humus line.

One burial was found, located at the approximate center of the mound, which consisted of the remains of four individuals (Fig. 4a). The burial had been made in a small oval pit dug below the mound floor. The dead were buried in the flesh in a flexed position. The remains were in a poor state of preservation, and age and sex could not be determined.

A stone altar was uncovered 3.5 feet southeast of Burial 1. The altar consisted of several burned sandstone boulders. Unburned sandstone and limestone rocks were scattered throughout the mound fill.

Mound 3 (Fig. 3c)

A low conical 28 feet in diameter with a maximum height of 1.6 feet. This mound had been pitted in the center and on the northwest side by earlier investigators. The mound was not stratified and no humus line was apparent.

One bundle reburial was located in a circular, bowl-like pit below the level of the mound floor (Fig. 5). This burial consisted of the remains of three individuals in fair condition: one female 18-21 years old and two adults of indeterminate sex. A few fragments of bones above this burial seem to indicate that a burial had been removed during the earlier pitting operation.

A stone altar of burned sandstone and containing charcoal and particles of burned bone was discovered on the mound floor 10 feet north of the burial. A cluster of hearth stones was also found above the mound floor, as well as a few pieces of standstone and limestone scattered through the mound fill at the same level (Fig. 4b).

Mound 4 (Fig. 3d)

This conical mound had a diameter of 25 feet and a maximum height of approximately 2 feet. In construction it was similar to Mound 1, being built of the same type of soil and showing no stratification. However, the old humus line was faintly apparent in some places.

A fully flexed burial representing the remains of a middle-aged adult male was found in a circular, sub-floor pit near the center of the mound (Figs. 6a, 7). The skull, which was fairly well preserved, indicated a lack of cradle-board deformation. The remaining parts of the skeleton were in very poor condition.

An earthen altar was located directly above the burial, a few inches up from the mound floor. Two altars (Fig. 6b) of burned limestone fragments were found, one 5 feet north, the other 2.5 feet east of the burial pit. Both were situated at the same level as the earthen fire area.

Fig. 4.   a. Burial, Mound 2; b. Scattered Stones, Mound 3 (MPM Negs. 408286. 408269).

Fig. 5. Burial, Mound 3 (MPM Neg. 408285).

Fig. 6.   a. Burial, Mound 4; b. Stone Altar, Mound 4 (MPM Negs. 408282, 408289).

Fig. 7. Broken Pottery Vessel, Mound 4 (MPM Neg. 408296).

Mound 7 (Fig. 8a)

A linear mound 80 feet long, 15 feet in width, with a maximum height of approximately 6 feet. The mound was constructed of grayish, clay-like soil containing an element of white-colored mold. No stratification was apparent, nor could a humus line be discovered beneath the mound. The mound was built on the natural land surface.

One burial was found lying in an elliptical, sub-floor pit. The bones were in such poor state of preservation that it was impossible to determine age, sex, or manner of burial.

A cluster of small limestone rocks was located above the mound floor, directly over the burial pit. They showed no evidence of having been burned.

Mound 8 (Fig. 8b)

A conical mound 27 feet in diameter and 3.5 feet in maximum height. The soil of which the mound was constructed was similar to that of Mound 1. No humus line was apparent. The mound was built on the natural land surface and was unstratified.

One burial was found which consisted of the poorly preserved remains of two adults, one male and one indeterminate, buried in the flesh in a flexed position, included in the fill above the mound floor (Fig. 9a).

One small altar, made of pieces of sandstone and limestone, was located above the mound floor 5 feet east of the burial.

Mound 10 (Fig. 8c)

This mound was of the type known as a bird effigy. It resembles a bird lying back up with wings extended. The maximum length from wing tip to wing tip was 130 feet, body length was 55 feet, and maximum height 3.5 feet above the surrounding ground surface. The mound was constructed of loamy soil, light brown with gray mottling, on dull reddish clay. No humus line could be seen and stratification was absent. The mound was built on the natural land surface.

One burial was recovered lying in an oval, sub-floor pit at approximately the center of the mound. The bones were so poorly preserved that it was impossible to gather any data from it.

A small stone altar was found on the mound floor 15 feet from the burial pit, in what would constitute the head of the bird.

Mound 11 (Fig. 8d)

A canine effigy 110 feet long from nose to tail, 43 feet wide at the broadest point including the legs, and 1.2 feet high at the highest point. The mound was not stratified nor was a humus line apparent.

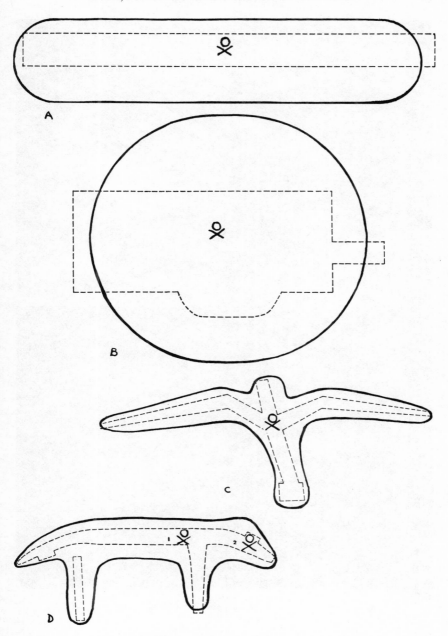

Fig. 8.   Raisbeck Group: a. Mound 7 ; b. Mound 8 ; c. Mound 10 ; d. Mound 11.

Fig. 9.   a. Burial, Mound 8; b. Burial, Mound 18 (MPM Negs. 408293, 408341).

Two burials were recovered, both being apparent only through discoloration of the soil. Burial 1 lay in an elliptical sub-floor pit at a point which would have marked the heart of the animal. Burial 2 was also made in a sub-floor pit of the same shape and was located in the approximate center of the animal's head.

No other interior features were found with the exception of a series of unburned stones scattered through the mound fill about the regions of the heart, shoulders, hips, and tail of the effigy figure.

Mound 18 (Fig. 10a)

A linear mound 122 feet in length, 17 feet in maximum width, and with a height of 2 feet at the highest point. No humus line nor stratification was apparent. The mound was constructed on the natural land surface.

A burial was found in an elliptical sub-floor pit 33 feet from the south end of the mound (Fig. 9b). The remains were those of a young adult male buried

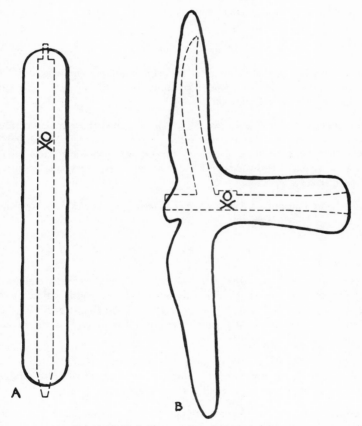

Fig. 10. Raisbeck Group: a. Mound 18; b. Mound 23.

in the flesh in a flexed position. The bones were poorly preserved and the age and sex assessments are, therefore, questionable.

A few medium-sized rocks were found scattered through the mound fill at each extremity of the mound. No other internal features were recovered.

Mound 23 (Fig. 10b)

This bird effigy had a wing spread of 138 feet, a body length of 63 feet, and a maximum elevation of approximately 1.2 feet. No humus line was present. The mound was built on the natural land surface and was not stratified.

One bundle reburial was discovered lying in an oblong, sub-floor pit located in the body just below the point where the wings are joined to the body of the bird. (Fig. 11a). The remains were those of a young adult, possibly female.

An earthen altar was uncovered which was situated above the mound floor, 12 feet from the tail end of the mound.

Mound 24 (Fig. 12a)

A conical mound with a diameter of 55 feet and a maximum height of 2.3 feet. The mound was not stratified and no humus line was apparent. Construction took place on the natural land surface.

One bundle reburial was recovered which contained the remains of four individuals. The bones had been placed directly on the mound floor. Although the remains were in a poor state of preservation, it was possible to determine that the burial consisted of two children of indeterminate sex, one young adult female, and one old female.

A group of limestone rocks had been placed over and nearly covering the burial (Fig. 13). No other interior mound features were found.

Mound 31 (Fig. 12b)

A bird effigy with extended wings which measured 150 feet from tip to tip through the center of the wings. The body was 68 feet in length with a maximum elevation of 2.7 feet. The mound was constructed of soil characteristic of the site. No humus line nor stratification could be defined. The mound lay on the natural land surface.

One bundle reburial, comprising the remains of two adults of indeterminate sex, was located in the approximate center of the body of the bird effigy. The individuals had been buried in an elliptical, sub-floor pit.

Interior features of the mound included a small earthen altar 5 feet west of the burial, and a stone altar located in the left wing 27 feet north of the burial.

Fig. 11. a. Burial, Mound 23 ; b. Burial, Mound 40 (MPM Negs. 409030, 408325).

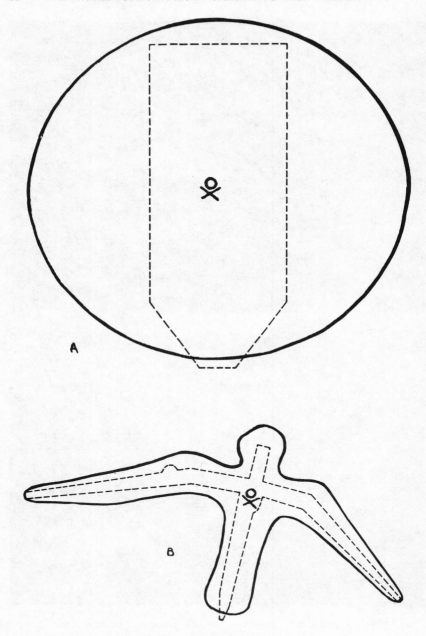

Fig. 12. Raisbeck Group : a. Mound 24 ; b. Mound 31.

Fig. 13. Stones With Burial, Mound 24 (MPM Neg. 409034).

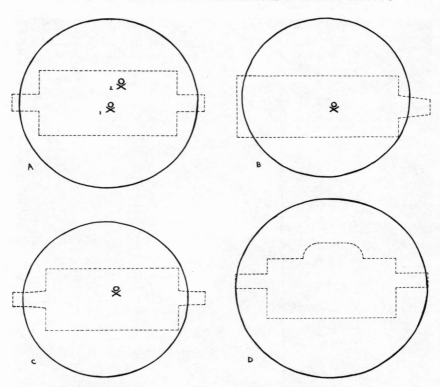

Fig. 14.   Raisbeck Group: a. Mound 38; b. Mound 39; c. Mound 40; d. Mound 42.

Mound 38 (Fig. 14a)

This was a conical mound with a diameter of 26 feet and a maximum elevation of less than 1 foot. The character of the soil was similar to that of Mound 1.
No humus line or stratification was visible and the mound was built on the
natural surface of the ground.

The remains of two burials were found. Burial 1 was a bundle reburial included in the mound fill a few inches above the floor at the approximate center
of the mound. The bones were poorly preserved and no data concerning the
individuals contained in it could be gathered. Burial 2, which lay 4 feet north
of Burial 1, was to be seen merely as discoloration in the soil.

A small earthen altar was situated slightly above the floor 13 feet northeast
of Burial 1. This feature consisted of a circular area approximately 1 foot in
diameter in which charcoal and ash were mixed with the soil.

Mound 39 (Fig. 14b)

A conical mound 27 feet in diameter with an elevation of less than 1 foot at
the highest point. The humus line was presumably removed before construction

began since the mound was built directly on yellow clay. No stratification was apparent.

One bundle reburial was recovered above the level of the mound floor, but the bones were so poorly preserved as to render identification impossible.

Two earthen altars were situated near the center of the mound close to the mound floor.

Mound 40 (Fig. 14c)

A conical mound 25 feet in diameter with a maximum height of less than 1 foot. The soil used in mound construction was similar to that of Mound 1 excepting an increased element of clay. The mound was not stratified and no humus line could be determined.

A bundle reburial containing parts of two individuals of indeterminate age and sex was found in the mound fill, above the level of the floor, near the center of the structure (Fig. 11b).

No interior features, other than stones scattered throughout the fill, were recognized.

Mound 42 (Fig. 14d)

This conical mound was 30 feet in diameter and 3.9 feet high at the highest point. The fill was a grayish brown, mold-impregnated clay soil which rested on pale yellow clay containing fragments of limestone. The humus had been removed below the mound and no stratification could be detected.

The central feature of this mound was an irregular dome of burned clay which extended over an area roughly 7 feet by 8 feet (Fig. 15a). This burned-clay area was between 1 and 2 feet thick and ranged in color from buff to brick red. The consistency in some places was as hard as brick, and in others very soft. Scattered through the mass were areas of dark brown, humus-colored earth, mottled somewhat with ash-gray and brown spots (Fig. 15b). Occasional round, black cross-sections of charcoal indicated the presence of charred posts running in various directions. One long pole seems to have extended northwest and southeast entirely through the center of the feature. A heavy layer of limestone occurred under the feature, and fragments were occasionally scattered through it. Bits of charcoal and burned animal bones were found throughout. Discoloration of the soil centrally below the feature may have indicated the presence of a former burial. However, nothing remained which could make burial identification positive.

Mound 55 (Fig. 16a)

An oval mound 30 feet long, 17 feet in width, and approximately 2 feet high at the highest point. The mound was unstratified and no humus line was visible.

Fig. 15.   a. Irregular Clay Dome, Mound 42 ; b. Cross-section through Clay Dome, Mound 42
(MPM Negs. 408333, 408337).

The only feature contained in this mound was a circular, sub-floor pit, 2.9 feet in diameter, which contained charcoal and other material resembling decayed organic matter. The latter was possibly the remains of a burial. The pit was located at the approximate center of the mound.

Mound 64 (Fig. 16b)

A conical mound 25 feet in diameter with a maximum height of 1.6 feet. The soil used in mound construction was typical of the site. No humus line was discernible and the mound was not stratified. Construction took place on the natural land surface.

One bundle reburial was found included in the fill slightly above the mound floor (Fig. 17a). It was established that six individuals were represented. These

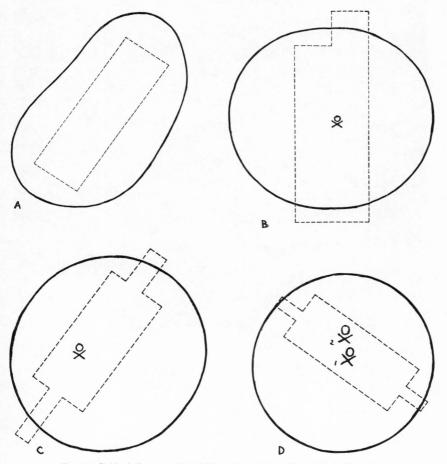

Fig. 16. Raisbeck Group: a. Mound 55; b. Mound 64; c. Mound 65; d. Mound 66.

Fig. 17.   a. Burial, Mound 64 ; b. Dog Burial, Mound 65 (MPM Negs. 409022, 409122).

were: five adults (two male, three indeterminate) and one child. Ages ranged as follows: one child, one young adult, three adults, and one old adult.

Scattered in a circle about the burial was a series of limestone fragments. No other interior mound features were found.

Mound 65 (Fig. 16c)

This conical mound was 37 feet in diameter and approximately 5 feet high at the point of greatest elevation. The soil used in construction was similar to that of Mound 1. No stratification or humus line could be determined.

One burial was recovered from the central area of the mound floor. This was a multiple bundle reburial composed of three main bundles (Fig. 18). Bundle 1 contained the remains of two children and one adult; Bundle 2, two adults, and

TABLE 2
EXTERNAL MEASUREMENTS OF UNEXCAVATED
RAISBECK GROUP MOUNDS
Effigy Mounds

Kind	Mound Number	Maximum length in feet	Maximum width in feet
Bird	12	150	70
Canine	13	130	48
Bird	27	180	64
Canine	28	98	43
Bird	29	175	82
Canine	33	67	30
Canine	34	97	39
Canine	35	98	34
Bird	48	65	45
Bird	49	68	40
Bird	50	95	55
Canine	52	120	60
Bird	53	100	48
Bird	56	100	55
Canine	59	88	37
Canine	63	80	42
Canine	67	132	40
Canine	69	50	23
Bird	75	85	48
Bird	83	110	43
Problematical	85	65	20

Fig. 18. Multiple Burial, Mound 65 (MPM Neg. 410003).

Bundle 3, one adult. The latter bundle had a stemmed end-scraper and a perforator associated with it. All of the bones were in a poor state of preservation.

Twelve feet east of the burial was the skeleton of a dog, complete except for the tail, lying on its right side on the floor of the mound (Fig. 17b). A small stone altar was situated 5 feet west of the burial, a few inches above the mound floor.

Mound 66 (Fig. 16d, 20)

A conical mound 35 feet in diameter with a maximum height of 2.6 feet. The mound was built of soil typical of the site. No humus line or mound stratification was visible.

Burial 1 was a large multiple bundle reburial which contained the remains of thirty-five individuals (Fig. 19). It was apparent that all the bones were deposited at one time. The burial was made by placing the bundles of bones together on the ground a few inches above the mound floor and covering them with fill. One of the bundles in this group had been partially cremated.

Burial 2 was a bundle reburial partially cremated. The remains had been placed in an oblong, sub-floor pit. The bones of both burials were badly preserved.

Two pottery pipes and a squared, turtle-plastron "mesh-spreader" were associated with Burial 1. No other interior features were uncovered.

TABLE 3
EXTERNAL MEASUREMENTS OF UNEXCAVATED RAISBECK GROUP MOUNDS

Linear Mounds

Mound Number	Maximum Length	Maximum Width
19	126 N-S	15
26	80 N-S	17
30	97 N-E S-W	16
32	92 N-E S-W	15
36	97 N-W S-E	14
46	105 N-W S-E	15
47	98 N-E S-W	14
54	104 N-W S-E	13
57	105 N-W S-E	14
62	158 N-E S-W	30
74	85 N-E S-W	22
78	130 N-E S-W	15

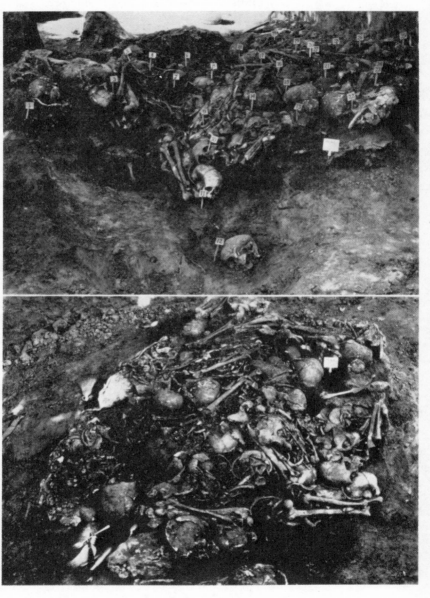

Fig. 19. a. and b. Multiple Burial, Mound 66 (MPM Negs. 409010, 409013).

TABLE 4
EXTERNAL MEASUREMENTS OF UNEXCAVATED
RAISBECK GROUP MOUNDS

Oval Mounds

Mound Number	Maximum Length	Maximum Width
79	27 N-W S-E	16
80	30 N-S	16.5

TABLE 5
EXTERNAL MEASUREMENTS OF UNEXCAVATED
RAISBECK GROUP MOUNDS

Conical Mounds

Mound Number	Maximum Diameter	Minimum Diameter
5	27 E-W	26.5
6	25 N-S	22.5
9	32 E-W	30
15	18 N-S	17.5
16	27 N-S	22.5
20	27.5 N-S	22.5
21	28 N-S	22.5
22	27.5 N-S	26
25	25 E-W	26.5
37	27.5 N-S	25
41	25 N-S	24.5
43	25 E-W	22.5
44	27.5 N-S	23
45	31.5 N-S	28.5
58	25.5 N-S	25
60	27.5 N-S	26
61	27 E-W	22.5
68	30 N-S	28
71	27.5 N-S	26
72	26.5 E-W	22.5
73	27.5 N-S	26
76	28 N-S	25
81	25.5 E-W	25
82	29 E-W	27.5
84	25 N-S	23

Fig. 20. Mound 66, Restored (MPM Neg. 409976).

POTTERY

A total of 445 rim and body sherds were found in the mounds of the Raisbeck Group. These can be broken down as follows:

TABLE 6
SHERD TOTALS ACCORDING TO SURFACE TREATMENT

Surface Treatment	Rim Sherds	Body Sherds
Cord-wrapped paddle		146
Smoothed-over CWP	7	169
Plain Surface	4	93
Single Cord Impressions	7	9
Rocked-Dentate Stamp		10

All the sherds are grit-tempered with a paste of reddish clay. The majority were found under such circumstances as to be considered as associated with the mound. However, a few, such as those with a roulette decoration, as well as the greater number of the plain-surfaced sherds, were scattered through the fill of the mounds (Fig. 21).

The smaller number of rim sherds makes it difficult to determine much about vessel shape. The smoothed-over cord-roughened rim sherds range in thickness from 5mm. to 13mm., and most of them have single cord impressions on the inside of the lip.

Fig. 21. Pottery Surface Decorations, Raisbeck Site (MPM Neg. 426932).

PIPES

Two pottery pipes were found. These were untempered, elbow-type pipes with simple incised lines around the rim of the bowl (Fig. 22).

The pottery types set up by McKern (1928, pp. 266-71) are not applicable here since all sherds have the same paste and temper and no fragments of polished ware were encountered.

STONE OBJECTS

The stone objects from the site were all manufactured by the chipping technique with the exception of four small abrading stones found in the mound fill. Since objects of this type have not been noted in effigy mounds but are found on occasion in the small campsites near the mounds, we can assume that those recovered at the Raisbeck site were accidentally included in the fill of the mounds during the time of construction.

PROJECTILE POINTS

Thirty-six projectile points were encountered during excavation. Of this number, ten were fragmentary and could not be classified. The remaining twenty-six fall into two main groups: (1) stemmed, and (2) notched. The latter category can be broken down further into side-notched and corner-notched points (Fig. 23).

The stemmed points were the most numerous; eighteen of them occurred at the site. They range in length from 44mm. to 78mm. Five side-notched points were found. These were more nearly of a size since the range in length was 56.5mm. to 69mm. Only three corner-notched projectile points were recovered. These showed the greatest variation in length, running from 22mm. to 67mm.

The points, including the fragments, were large, coarse, roughly chipped implements exhibiting little secondary chipping or retouching.

PERFORATORS

Three chipped-stone drills or perforators were found in association with features or burials in the mounds. They are slender, pointed tools with an expanded base or hafting end. The general workmanship indicates fine control in chipping, especially when contrasted to the more massive projectile points.

BONE OBJECTS

Few bone artifacts were discovered in the Raisbeck mounds. This is not surprising in view of the generally poor condition of the bone in the burials. No doubt such bone implements as were deposited in the mounds have, for the most part, long since disintegrated. Two objects of bone and one of antler were recovered. One bone awl made from the leg bone of a fairly large bird, one

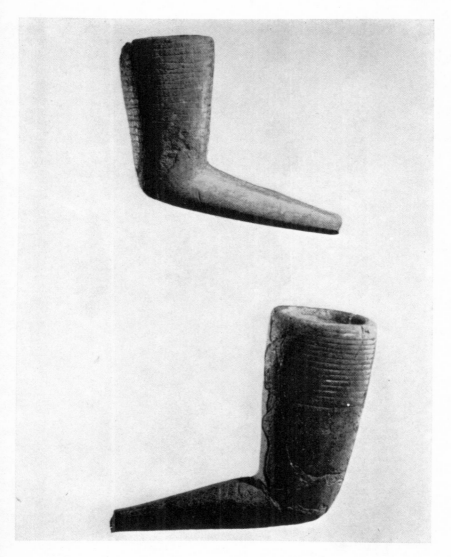

Fig. 22. Pottery Pipes, Raisbeck Site (MPM Neg. 426929).

Fig. 23. Projectile Points, Raisbeck Site (MPM Neg. 426938).

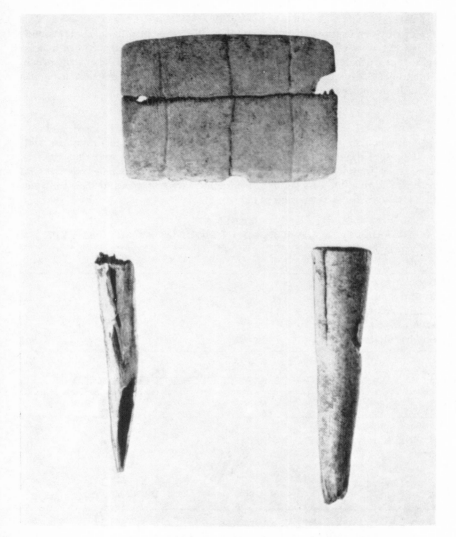

Fig. 24. "Mesh-spreader," Bone Awl, and Antler Handle, Raisbeck Site (MPM Neg. 426935).

"mesh-spreader" made of a portion of turtle plastron, and one antler tip cut and reamed for use as a large projectile point of socketed handle (Fig. 24).

DISPOSAL OF THE DEAD

Eighteen burials were found in the Raisbeck Group (Table 7, p. 48). Of this number four were single flesh burials, two were multiple flesh burials, six were multiple bundle reburials, and four were indeterminate. No single bundle reburials were encountered.

INTERIOR MOUND FEATURES

Twenty-one features (Tables 8 and 9, p. 48), other than burials, were found; all but two were ceremonial fireplaces or altars. Two features, classified as miscellaneous, include a dog burial and an unusual clay, dome-like structure in Mound 42. All interior features occurred in conical or bird mounds, none was found in the other mound types represented at the site.

SKELETAL REMAINS

The skeletal material from the Raisbeck site has not been restored, and consequently no data regarding physical type is forthcoming at this time. In addition, much of the material of this class was too badly eroded to permit analysis. The skulls from Mound 66, which contained the large bundle reburial and promised to yield the best samples, are fragmentary or warped to such an extent that measurement is not meaningful.

TABLE 7
DISTRIBUTION OF BURIALS IN MOUNDS BY MOUND TYPE

Burial Type	Conical	Bird	Linear	Canine	Oval
Single, flesh	1	1	2		
Multiple flesh	2				
Single, reburial					
Multiple, reburial	7	1			
Indeterminate		1	1	1	1

TABLE 8
DISTRIBUTION OF SINGLE FEATURES IN MOUNDS

Mound Type	Mound Number	Altar	Miscellaneous
Conical	2	1	
Conical	8	1	
Bird	10	1	
Bird	23	1	
Conical	38	1	
Conical	42		Clay dome

TABLE 9
DISTRIBUTION OF MULTIPLE FEATURES IN MOUNDS

Mound Type	Mound Number	Altar	Miscellaneous
Conical	1	4	
Conical	3	2	
Conical	4	3	
Bird	31	2	
Conical	39	2	
Conical	65	1	Dog burial

Chapter III

GENERAL DESCRIPTION OF THE EFFIGY MOUND CULTURE OF WISCONSIN

COMMUNITY LIFE

The builders of the effigy mounds of Wisconsin have left behind no evidence of permanent habitation. At some of the mound groups small, thin, scattered deposits of generalized potsherds, a few flint chips, and an occasional stone artifact have been assessed as Effigy Mound culture campsites. This tendency to so classify them is due more to the geographical proximity to the mound groups than to any actual archaeological associations. In most instances where such campsites occur, the dwelling areas have been disturbed by the actual mound building. Soil and refuse material from their middens have been included in some of the mounds. This fact indicates that certain of the mounds in a group of this kind are of more recent origin than the camp areas. It does not mean that all the mounds of a given group are more recent, however, since it is believed that in no group were all the mounds built at one time. The campsites and the mounds often have certain traits in common, but these are usually of a very general nature and not diagnostic of Effigy Mound. In addition, certain traits occur in the campsites which are not found in the mounds. These include artifacts such as stone axes (three-quarter grooved and an occasional fluted ax) ; abrading stones of sandstone or rough limestone; hammerstones; and fragments of pottery, grit-tempered, with notched lips, and decorated with sharp, thin-line incising. All of these traits, except for the fluted ax, are exceedingly generalized, particularly the stone objects which can be duplicated in almost every archaeological province in North America. Whereas it is possible that the dwelling areas situated near the mound groups do represent temporary campsites of the mound builders, this remains an inference and, so far as the writer is aware, no village or camp midden has at present been definitely demonstrated to represent the remains of an Effigy Mound community.

Baerreis (pp. 5-19) calls the Black Hawk Village Site an Effigy Mound village. This association is tenuous, however, as it is based on a type of pottery which is found in effigy mounds but which cannot be considered diagnostic of the culture since it has a wide distribution outside Effigy Mound.

We are left with the fact that no village, either near or farther removed from the mound groups, has been associated culturally with the mounds themselves. We may assume, therefore, that the Effigy Mound people were a semisedentary population who did not live in one place long enough to build up heavy midden deposits. Such a conclusion might justify characterization of them as primarily a hunting and gathering people. This question will be discussed at greater length later in this study.

ECONOMIC LIFE

A consideration of the artifacts found to be associated with the mounds of this culture adds support to the premise that the Effigy Mound peoples were mainly food gatherers and hunters. Articles of stone, bone, antler, and shell, as well as pottery, occur in varying frequencies. These will be discussed first simply in a descriptive manner, and then put together in the light of an attempt to discover functional implications.

Stone Objects

Chipped Stone

Most of the artifacts produced by chipping are rather large, heavy, and coarse. Percussion rather than pressure flaking is the common technique and would, of course, account for this fact. Chipped-stone objects are made of impure chert and quartzite which correspond to local materials (Fig. 25).

A. *Projectile points.* Objects of this class, which includes both arrow and spear points, are the most common of the chipped-stone implements. They occur, for the most part, in various stemmed and notched types. (The term "for the most part" is used because some of them are fragmentary, and the form cannot be readily determined.) The stemmed points tend to be approximately the same in size, the variation in length ranging from 55mm. to 60mm. The notched points, however, show a much wider range in length, varying from 25mm. to 93mm. That some of the larger points would make cumbersome arrow points is the assumption that leads to the inclusion of spear points in the trait list, although it is by no means certain that some of the smaller ones did not serve such a function also. Leaf-shaped points are rare.

B. *Scrapers.* Both side- and end-scrapers are characteristic of the Effigy Mound culture. The side-scrapers do not conform to any particular type, but can be described as very heavy and generalized. In outline, they are roughly curved and the scraping edges exhibit large, rough flake scars with no finer secondary chipping. The end-scrapers occur in both the stemmed and notched forms and appear to have been fashioned from reworked projectile points, presumably those which had been broken, or rejected in manufacture.

C. *Perforators.* The chipped-stone perforators or drills exhibit the finest chipping to be found on Effigy Mound stone objects. The base is variously "winged" or expanded and the blade is generally a thin, elongated point roughly diamond-shaped in cross-section.

Pecked, Ground, and Polished Stone

Implements in this category may exhibit one or another or any combination of these techniques. Objects produced in these ways are not as common as those manufactured by the technique of chipping (Fig. 26).

A. *Spuds* (also known as "handled celts"). These objects are characterized by a rough to partially or wholly smoothed surface, tapered tang, and a

Fig. 25. Chipped-stone Objects, Effigy Mound Culture (MPM Neg. 426936).

Fig. 26.   Ground-stone Objects, Effigy Mound Culture (MPM Neg. 426937).

flat, ovoid head. They are not common in mounds of the Effigy Mound culture; in fact, only thirty-two have been definitely reported from Wisconsin. However, relative to this McKern (1928, p. 260) says, "It is noteworthy that the Wisconsin area in which spuds have been found is bounded on the south by the Illinois line, on the west by Sauk County, on the east by Lake Michigan, and on the north by Door County, an area roughly comparable to the effigy mound area, though more limited."

B. *Stone axes.* Pecked and ground stone axes are mentioned here because there has been a tendency to list the fluted axe as a diagnostic trait of the Effigy Mound culture. Actually no stone axes have been found in the mounds proper. A few three-quarter grooved axes have been found at campsites near the mounds, but, as was mentioned earlier, it has not been demonstrated that the campsites represent the Effigy Mound culture. The fluted axe, so called because of the grooves which usually run parallel to the length of the axe along the blade, is merely assumed to be Effigy Mound because its distribution quite closely coincides with the distribution of the mounds. No specimen has been found definitely associated with the mounds.

C. *Celts.* Pecked and partially ground celts are all single-bitted objects with a tapered poll. Although the shape is constant, they range in size from 31mm. in width and 66mm. in length to 54mm. in width and 110mm. in length. Only five specimens have been reported.

D. *Stone "Saws."* These are pieces of slate of irregular shape which have tiny serrations on one or more edges. Three have been found associated with this culture. One of these, a long, thin, pointed piece measures 220mm. in length by 52mm. in width. McKern (1928, p. 260) states, "Implements of this type have been generally called, in this province, stone saws. Whether they were actually used as saws, specialized scrapers, or in some other capacity, they are of rare occurrence in Wisconsin. . . . The fact that four of the exceedingly limited number of these artifacts which have come to light in Wisconsin are from the Buffalo Lake district, three being found at a single site where they marked the focal points in conical mounds, may prove of interest. The series of data is so small, however, that little of scientific importance can be ascribed to it."

Bone and Antler Objects (Fig. 27)

A. *Bone awls.* The most common type of bone awl is fashioned from the ulna of the deer. Only the shaft is split and pointed; the proximal end is left unmodified. Splinter awls are present, but are not as common. Two specimens which are long and narrow with a circular cross-section, and worked on all surfaces, have been reported. This is the type known variously as a bone skewer, bone pin, or needle without an eye.

B. *Bone "harpoon" points.* These "harpoons" are worked on all sides and occur with varying numbers of barbs. Complete specimens with as few as four barbs and as many as ten have been recovered. The barbs always occur on one

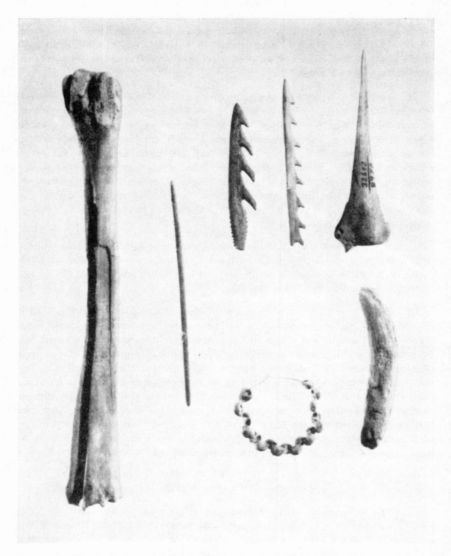

Fig. 27. Bone and Shell Objects, Effigy Mound Culture (MPM Neg. 426933).

side only. One four-barbed specimen, which measures 90mm. in length, had small notches or serrations along both sides of the base which may have served to facilitate shafting. There is an apparent difference in the manner in which the Effigy Mound "harpoons" are made as compared with those found at Aztalan, in southern Wisconsin. The Aztalan "harpoons" are rough in the spaces between the barbs, indicating that the bone was sawed out in two or three successive cuts, whereas the Effigy Mound "harpoons" are smooth on all surfaces, including the area cut out to form the barbs.

C. *Bone beamers.* Only two bone scrapers or beamer-type tools are known from Effigy Mound sites. These were found with one skeleton in a compound burial. They were made from the cannon bone of a deer by cutting out an elliptical slot on one side of the bone. Both specimens exhibit polishing on the working edges which occurs through use.

D. *Worked bear toes.* These cut and perforated bear toe bones have been listed by McKern and Ritzenthaler (p. 44) as part of a cup-and-pin game. Functional names such as "dangles" and other terms implying ornamentation have also been applied to them. Since there is little direct evidence in any case, they fall into the classification of problematical objects.

E. *"Mesh spreaders."* Another problematical category. Very possibly these squared pieces of turtle plastron were used in net making and functioned as spacers to produce a net of uniform mesh. The one specimen known, from the Raisbeck site, measures 70mm. by 50mm.

F. *Antler objects.* The most common antler artifacts are the flakers made from an antler tine. These all show evidence of use at the tip and are made either by simply breaking off the tine or by cutting. Knife marks are apparent on some of them. A few antler tips have been recovered which show evidence of being worked on all surfaces and drilled out at the base. They may represent antler projectile points or socketted handles. Presumably both are present, but it is difficult to determine which is which.

Shell Objects (Fig. 27)

The only objects of shell recovered from the mounds are hemispherical beads simply made by grinding off one side of the anculosa shell, a procedure which produces two holes on a single flat surface.

Metal Objects (Fig. 28)

Copper was the only metal employed by the effigy mound builders, and all objects were made by cold hammering of native copper, or with the aid of annealing at low-fire temperatures. To date, only two types of copper tools have been found in association with this culture, namely, the celt or wedge-like implement and the awl. Both kinds are rare. The celts are flat, parallel-sided, rectangular objects with a bit at one end and a flat striking surface at the other. They range in length from 90mm. to 99mm. and in width from 29mm. to 33mm. The copper awls are slender, double-pointed tools with a square cross-section.

Fig. 28. Copper Objects, Effigy Mound Culture (MPM Neg. 426931).

Pottery

The pottery described here is that which is found to be definitely associated with the Effigy Mound culture and does not, therefore, include all pottery that occurs in the mound fill. The process of scooping up dirt for mound construction results in the inclusion in the mound of sherds of former occupation at the areas from which the dirt was taken. As a result, it cannot be positively ascertained that such pottery belongs to the Effigy Mound assemblage. The presence of these accidentally included sherds would serve to give some idea of the chronological relationship of Effigy Mound and other Wisconsin cultural manifestations, if, for example, shell-tempered pottery fragments were introduced into a mound in this manner. However, only one instance of a chronological hint of this type has been recorded. This will be discussed in a later part of this report.

It might be well to state at the outset that the pottery generally associated with this culture is exceedingly generalized and it becomes difficult to break it down into types that have meaning. It is considered more expedient here to make general statements about it and to indicate, in addition, the variations which occur, rather than attempt to establish a series of types that would be difficult to use and which would have to be added to each time a variance in surface treatment was noted.

The pottery is Woodland in tradition. McKern (1930, p. 469) has assigned it to a large class of pottery which he calls Lake Michigan ware. This ware includes the pottery of the Effigy Mound type but is so generalized and has a distributional range of such a nature that it cannot be considered diagnostic of the Effigy Mound culture.

The primary technique employed in pottery manufacture here is the so-called paddle-and-anvil method, although some coiling does occur. In fact, some specimens appear to have been made by a combination of both. The pottery is characteristically soft and porous with a granular paste. Consequently, it is most often poorly preserved, and method of manufacture is difficult to determine in many instances. The paste of the pottery vessels is a coarse, reddish clay tempered with grit material, usually a partially disintegrated granite or crushed quartz. All exterior surfaces show treatment with a cord-wrapped paddle, generally considered to be a functional as well as a decorative technique which tends to compress the clay and cause the walls of the vessel to be strengthened as a result. In some cases these cord impressions have been partially smoothed over; however, the marks are still faintly discernible. Completely plain- or smooth-surface sherds have been reported from the Raisbeck Group only, where they constitute about one-fifth of all the pottery found. However, whole pots are generally not cord marked on the base, and these may be primarily basal sherds. Polished-surface sherds are extremely rare to absent; McKern (1928, pp. 270-71) describes a single sherd with this treatment.

The few complete pots and the larger rim and basal sherds indicate that there is but one vessel shape for Effigy Mound pottery (Figs. 29, 30, 31). This is a rather small pot with a fairly open mouth and a wide shoulder which has a

Fig. 29. Pottery Vessel, Effigy Mound Culture (MPM Neg. 7961).

Fig. 30. Pottery Vessel, Effigy Mound Culture (MPM Neg. 70140).

Fig. 31. Pottery Vessel, Effigy Mound Culture (MPM Neg. 401861).

tendency to slope away toward a conoidal base. Some variation relative to proportions does occur in this general shape.

The greatest variations, however, appear with regard to the shape of the rims and the manner of decoration placed over the cord-roughened surface (Fig. 32). Rims are low or medium and usually slightly out-flaring, although vertical rims do occur. More rarely the rim follows the line of the neck and has a tendency to be somewhat incurving. In most instances the lip is of the same thickness as the vessel wall, but occasionally the outer lip margin shows thickening. In a large percent of the cases, thickened lips are produced by folding the clay over rather than by application of a clay strip. A few collared vessels have been noted, an especially good example coming from the Nitschke site (McKern, 1930, Pl. LXVI).

The great majority of the Effigy Mound vessels are decorated, the design again showing considerable variation. All design elements are geometric in style and differ primarily in complexity. A simple design composed of straight lines forming a horizontal band around the upper part of the vessel is most frequent. A more complex and elaborate geometric type does occur, but is of less importance numerically than the simpler forms (Plate XXIII). Aside from the overall cord roughening, several techniques for producing decoration are recognizable.

1. *Imprinting with single cords.* This is by far the most commonly employed.
2. *Punctating.* Indentations made with a small, pointed implement.

Fig. 32. Pottery Surface Treatments, Effigy Mound Culture (MPM Neg. 426930).

3. *Puncturing or piercing.* This results in a series of holes which extend completely through the rim.
4. *Embossing.* Embossed nodes are produced by pressing a rounded implement into the wet clay from the interior of the vessel in such a manner as to cause the clay to be pushed out in a series of knobs or nodes on the exterior surface.
5. *Indentation.* A type of stamping done with a hollow reed, cut bone, or other natural object. These produce both circular and angular design elements. Rocked-dentate stamped sherds are rare, but this technique should be mentioned here with the category of indentation.
6. *Incising.* Both narrow and broad line incising occurs, generally following around the vessel horizontally rather than vertically.

All of these techniques are applied after the cord-wrapped paddle treatment has been completed.

Decoration is confined to the upper part of the vessel, usually covering the rim and lip, but occasionally extending to the shoulder. Decoration made by single cord impressions frequently occurs on the interior of the rim.

Pipes

Effigy Mound pipes are made of pottery. The elbow type, with a wide-mouthed, expanding bowl and short to medium, tapered stem, is typical (Figs. 33, 22). The angle of stem to bowl varies from approximately 30 to 90 degrees, the right-angle style being most common. The paste of the pipes differs from that of the pottery vessels in that it contains no tempering material of any kind. Decoration is not common, but when it does occur is similar in design to that employed on the pottery vessels, with the exception that there is not the great variation nor complexity of design that is to be found on the pots. McKern (1930, p. 467) says of the pipes, "The pottery pipes of the Effigy Mound culture . . . are so typically eastern Algonkian in material, workmanship, general style and detail, and variety of shape that it seems adequate to describe them as of known primitive Algonkian type.

When these artifacts are considered from the point of view of their probable function, some insight can be gained relative to the subsistence basis of the Effigy Mound people. The projectile points (both spear- and arrow-heads), the side- and end-scrapers, the awls (both copper and bone) would seem to argue for a hunting and hide-preparing economy. The "mesh spreaders," if indeed that is what they are, and the bone "harpoon" points suggest some fishing, although it is quite true that the functional identity of the square of turtle plastron is uncertain, and the "harpoons" may have been used for hunting smaller game animals. The point is that the artifacts (mainly tools) recovered through archaeological efforts and assigned to the Effigy Mound culture appear to be more in keeping with a hunting-fishing-gathering economy than with that of an agricultural group. No mortars, pestles, milling stones, hoes, or other equipment generally

Fig. 33. Pottery Pipes, Effigy Mound Culture (MPM Neg. 426934).

considered to be essential to the processing of crops have been discovered in association with the remains of this culture. It is possible, however, that agricultural artifacts were made of perishable material.

The presence of pipes might indicate a knowledge of tobacco cultivation, although not necessarily on a large scale, or even at all, for tobacco may have been obtained through trade. The Algonkians, for example, had the practice of smoking "kinnikinnick," of which several varieties were prepared either from young inner bark or leaves, or a mixture of this and tobacco. Thus a small crop of tobacco would last a considerable length of time. In addition, the knowledge of tobacco raising does not necessarily establish a knowledge and practice of cultivation of other plants for food. Other hunting groups are known to have raised tobacco in a limited amount, but did not grow food crops at all. Wissler (p. 31) says that ". . . the Black-foot and the Crow did not attempt any other agriculture except the raising of tobacco. . . ."

CEREMONIAL LIFE

It is difficult for the archaeologist to speak in an authoritative way about the more intangible aspects of an extinct culture. It is also difficult, in many instances, to conclusively assess the true function of a trait or complex of traits. Braidwood (pp. 108-12) has pointed out the various factors involved in the limitations of archaeology. There is a certain tendency to classify problematical items as "ceremonial" and, in addition, to carry over ideas and practices from the archaeologist's own culture to that of the earlier people with whose cultural remains he is working. This is not to say that such tendencies are invariably bad. They are not if they lead to standardization of terminology or some other useful purpose. Often no other interpretation is helpful. In general, burial practices of peoples all over the world are considered to be of ceremonial nature. It becomes more and more apparent that the mounds of Wisconsin which have given the Effigy Mound culture its name were built primarily as burial tumuli. Because this is the case and because many of them are of unusual shape, it is tempting to label them and their contents as evidence of the ceremonial life of the people who built and used them. We will accept, then, burial customs as being a part of the ceremonial life of this group. We will also find that the greatest percentage of our information regarding the Effigy Mound culture has to do with their methods of disposal of the dead.

Burial Mounds

Mounds

All burials recognized as belonging to the Effigy Mound culture occur in mounds. The mounds are low, probably never much more than 5 feet high originally and now somewhat lower due to natural erosion and farming activity carried on by present-day farmers. These structures are often of considerable length. The linear mounds, for example, may be more than 200 feet long. There is a marked variation in the size of mounds from site to site. The normal range in

Fig. 34. Typical Cists, Effigy Mound Culture (MPM Neg. 48117).

length (including the effigies) is roughly from about 60 to 300 feet, when the tail is included in the measurement, although in the extreme a length of 575 feet has been recorded.

The mound groups are generally located on high ground, ridges, or bluffs overlooking streams, rivers, or lakes. However, this is merely a general tendency and occasionally groups are reported in other locations. Thomas (1890, p. 532) points out:

"There appears to have been no rule in reference to the character of the ground by which the builders were governed in selecting the localities for their imitative works, as they are found on the level shore of Lake Michigan, on the gentle slopes that border the lakes about Madison, while at and around Prairie du Chien they are found on the bottoms subject to occasional overflow, up to the crests of the sharpest ridges which divide the drainage areas of the streams of that region. Nor is a level spot oftener selected than one that slopes to a greater or less degree. They occasionally occur on quite steep hillsides and on sharp crested spurs where the summit is so narrow as to necessitate lapping over from one side to the other. The preference of the builder, however, seems to have been for the highlands, especially those bordering upon the rivers and lakes. Even the summits of the high bluffs which flank the Mississippi were selected as the sites of the most complicated groups of effigies. As a general rule they are in groups or connected with groups, few being found wholly isolated; and even the groups of a given section, as Rev. S. D. Peet concludes, appear to have been arranged or located with reference to a village or tribal system of some kind."

No orientation of the mounds within a given location is apparent, although earlier writers convey the impression that the effigies of a particular group will always be oriented along the same axis and heading in the same direction. In addition, it was considered that the animals would be lying on the same side. McKern (1930, pp. 437-39) has shown that such is not the case when he points out, "Such alignment of mounds as occurs is logically explained as the result of parallel placement to natural ridges upon which the mounds are built."

And again, ". . . there is a general tendency for the effigy mounds of the Kletzien Group to head south with the legs extending toward the stream bank. Apropos to this orientation, the general slope of the land surface throughout the mound-occupied area is from northwest to southeast and from northeast to southwest; in other words, with the flow of the stream on the one hand and toward the near bank of the stream on the other."

Further, "Three of the panthers have legs represented as extending toward the east; the other two, toward the west. This lack of uniformity is readily explained, however, by the fact that the legs are always directed toward the downhill side. All those effigies on the western slope of the ridge have the legs extending westward; all those on the eastern slope have the legs extending eastward."

The mounds in any group vary considerably in numbers as well as in the shapes or types of mounds represented. A problem arises with regard to determining the numerical importance of the different shapes. This results from the fact that more than one specific name has been applied to the same shape. That certain shapes recur in the various mound groups throughout the State is apparent and a classification can be set up and the terms standardized, but at best such terminology is arbitrary. The problem has its roots in past decades for we read such statements as those of Lapham (p. 9), quoting Dr. P. R. Hoy of Racine, Wisconsin, as follows: ". . . bounded . . . on the west by a 'lizard mound' eighty feet long." A footnote states, "This appellation lizard is given for convenience to a class of mounds having two projections or legs on one side near the large extremity, without pretending that they are actually intended to represent lizards." This same class of mounds today is known as "panther" and it is presumed that the same convenience rather than actual appearance is intended. Again, the same confusion in terms is indicated in the statement of Cyrus Thomas (1890, p. 531).

"The supposed 'Man mounds' are most likely poor representations of swallow-tailed birds. The animals indicated by these peculiar works, so far as they can be indentified with reasonable certainty, pertain to the modern fauna of the district. The supposed exception to this rule—the so-called 'Elephant mound'— as proven by the evidence presented in the report of field work, was probably intended to represent a bear."

Such examples can be multiplied many times. Consequently, for the purposes of this report certain mound types and terms will be recognized for use in ordering data. In some instances, previously separate types will be grouped together. For example, mounds which have been termed "duck," "eagle," et cetera will be placed in the larger and more usable category of "bird mounds." Also included in the bird group are the two types sometimes called "cross" and "man" mounds. We will recognize, then, thirteen mound types in the Effigy Mound culture (Figs. 35, 36). These are as follows:

(1) Conical
(2) Oval
(3) Biconical
(4) Linear
(5) Panther
(6) Bear
(7) Bird
(8) Deer
(9) Buffalo
(10) Turtle
(11) Canine
(12) Beaver
(13) Problematical

The term "Problematical" represents a catch-all category into which are placed all of the mounds which, for any reason, cannot be identified as belonging

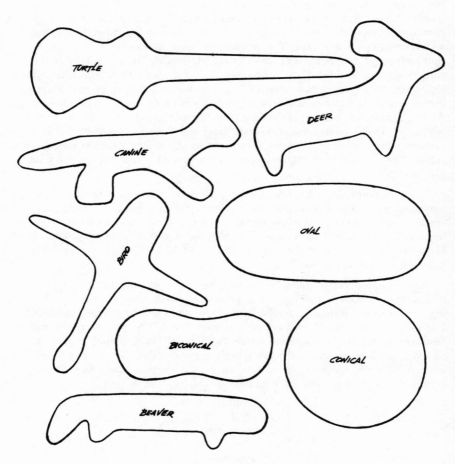

Fig. 35. Mound Types of the Effigy Mound Culture.

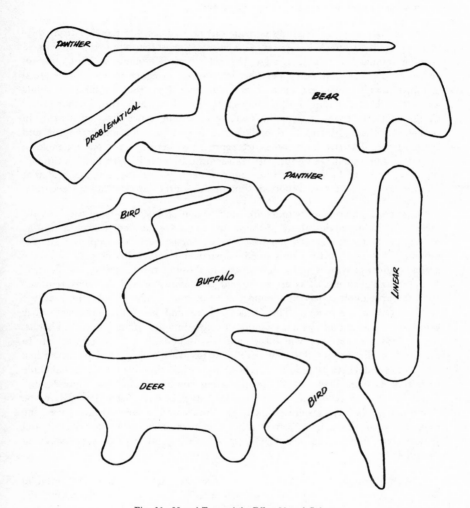

Fig. 36. Mound Types of the Effigy Mound Culture.

to any of the other types. Some of the mounds have been so badly eroded as to defy classification while others have simply been built in such a manner that resemblance to known species is not apparent.

As already stated, this study is made on the basis of 483 mounds from thirteen widely distributed, known sites. Analysis shows that these types occur in varying frequencies (Table 1, page 15). The conical mounds without question represent the most common type. The next largest category is the problematical group, although the linear mounds are almost as numerous. Panther mounds are in fourth place, numerically followed by bird, bear, and oval, in that order. Canine and deer mounds are next, and the remaining types drop off sharply in frequency. Biconical and turtle follow the deer type, and finally beaver and buffalo types. The two latter types are represented here by only one example in each case and would not be included as separate types if it were not for the fact that they seem to be fairly accurate representations of these animals, and that other examples have been reported, though the sources are not always accurate.

In every instance the mounds are built of soil scooped up from the immediately surrounding area. Many of these structures are mottled in such a way as to suggest that individual scoop or container loads were built up to form the mound. This is a feature of mound construction found in mounds of many archaeological provinces and is not unique in those of the Effigy Mound culture. In some of the groups it is apparent that the humus or sod line was removed from the area upon which the mound was to be built, a method of delimiting the areal extent of the mound. This is not a hard and fast rule, however. Other groups include mounds which contain so-called intaglio "foundations." That is, the earth at the spot upon which the mound is to be built is removed not only to the depth of the humus line, but additional excavation is carried on in such a way as to produce an intaglio or reverse cameo of the intended mound. This hole or outline is then filled in and the mounding continued until the "foundation" shape is achieved in mound form. Several intaglios have been reported in the State and it was first assumed that these represented unfinished structures, the foundations of which had been dug but the mounds never built (Barrett and Hawks, pp. 16-20). McKern (1930, pp. 459-60) questions this successfully in the statement :

"Such a premise would lead one to expect, at least to some extent, intaglio floors in mounds of groups where open intaglios are present. Therefore, the presence of an effigy intaglio at the Kletzien site rendered important a very careful and thorough examination of the floors of all the mounds excavated to determine the possible presence of intaglio floors. However, no evidence of any kind of mound floor depressions was found."

With the exception of the mounds of the Kratz Creek group, mound fill is unstratified. In no case is there any evidence to indicate that the mounds were built in successive stages. Each was apparently begun and finished within a rather short time.

Interior features, other than burials, have been found in all types of mounds with the exception of the canine and beaver forms. It is to be noted, however, that only three canine mounds and one beaver type have been excavated. It cannot be said that all mounds contain features of one sort or another, but it is true that features of the same type have been encountered in all mound forms, with the exceptions noted above. Most common of the interior features are the fireplaces or altars. These may appear simply as circular areas in the earth which show evidence of firemaking or as more elaborately constructed forms made of stones placed in a circular fashion. Altars may occur singly or in numbers as high as ten in an individual mound. (See charts 2, 3, and 4, Appendix, for distribution of these and other features according to mound type.) In general, these features occur directly over or very near burial pits and inclusive burials, or in prominent parts of the effigies such as the head, heart, et cetera.

Cists have a more limited distribution, being restricted to the conical, bear, and certain problematical forms. Numerically, however, they are as common as the altars.

Pits, aside from burial pits, are not common. Only two have been encountered and both of these occurred in conical mounds. In each instance, the pits contained nothing which would provide a clue as to their use. Other features are rare, and because of their specific nature and single occurrence have been placed in a miscellaneous category.

TABLE 10

TOTAL DISTRIBUTION OF FEATURES BY MOUND TYPE

Mound Type	Number of Features	Number Excavated
Conical	31	82
Oval	3	8
Biconical	3	6
Linear	2	24
Panther	5	9
Bear	6	10
Bird	2	8
Deer	2	1
Buffalo	1	2
Turtle	1	1
Beaver	0	1
Canine	0	3
Problematical	10	25

METHODS OF DISPOSAL OF THE DEAD

Three principal burial methods occur in the mounds of the Effigy Mound culture. These are: (1) burial of the body in the flesh immediately after death, (2) reburial of the bones of the dead after exposure and decomposition of the soft parts, and (3) cremation. Tabulation of the burials by type indicates a total of fifty-five each of flesh and reburials, and four cremations. Thirty-seven burials were so poorly preserved that they must be classified as indeterminate. All the flesh burials were flexed. The data are somewhat more enlightening when each type is broken down. The flesh burials can be considered to be of two kinds: (a) burial of a single individual in the flesh, and (b) burial of more than one individual in the flesh in the same grave (multiple flesh burials). No multiple flesh burial has been reported containing the remains of more than six persons and usually they do not exceed three or four. Distribution of these sub-types reveals that forty-seven of the total number were single flesh burials and only eight were multiple. The reburials can be broken down on the same basis: (a) reburials containing the bundled bones of a single individual, and (b) reburials consisting of the bundled bones of more than one individual (multiple reburials). The largest number of individuals reported for one multiple bundle reburial is forty-five, encountered in Mound 1 of the Kratz Creek Group (Barrett and Hawkes, pp. 35-45). One burial of this type containing thirty-five individual bundles was found in Mound 66 of the Raisbeck Group (p. 41). However, the usual number of individual bundles is considerably less than that. Figures on the distribution of these sub-types do not show a great difference in frequency— thirty-two single bundle reburials. Combinations of flesh and bundle reburials also occur. Only four cremations have been definitely established and in each case the bones were only partially, rather than completely, burned. Partial cremations of both flesh and bundle reburials have been observed (Chart 1, Appendix ix A).

Burials have been recovered from mounds of each of the thirteen types recognized here. Specific types of burials are not confined to specific mound forms since both flesh and bundle reburials occur in all types with the exception of the turtle, beaver, and canine mounds. It should be noted again that the sample for the latter types is small and future excavation may cause them to be included in the statement.

Location of burials in the mounds shows some variation. Three primary positions occur: (1) in circular or oblong pits dug below the floor of the mound, (2) burial placed directly on the mound floor, no pit, and (3) in the mound fill anywhere above the mound floor, again no pit. There is no apparent correlation between type of burial and position in the mound, although there is a tendency for flesh burials to be more numerous in the sub-floor pits. Both flesh and bundle reburials have been noted in each of the three places of disposal, however. In the event that a given mound contains only one burial, the usual location of that burial (whether sub-floor pit, floor, or fill) is in the center of the conical, oval, or linear mounds and at such points in the effigies as the head, region of the shoulders or heart, hips, or where the legs or wings join the body of the figure.

TABLE 11
TOTAL DISTRIBUTION OF BURIALS BY MOUND TYPE

Mound Type	Number of Burials	Number Excavated
Conical	56	82
Oval	11	8
Biconical	5	6
Linear	7	14
Panther	21	24
Bear	4	9
Bird	9	10
Deer	8	8
Buffalo	2	1
Turtle	4	2
Canine	2	2
Problematical	22	9

Mortuary furniture seldom accompanies the Effigy Mound burials. Such artifacts as are included with the body are of the usual type, and no objects which can be considered special grave goods, as distinguished from utilitarian artifacts, have been found. Most of the associated artifacts of Effigy Mound occur with the fireplaces, features of other types, or are found lying directly on the prepared floor of the mound.

SUMMARY TRAIT LIST FOR EFFIGY MOUND

I. Community Life.

Small temporary dwelling areas with thin, scattered midden deposits.

II. Economic Life

Hunting, fishing and gathering primary means of substance.

A. Artifacts

1. Chipped stone objects
   a. Stemmed and notched projectile points
   b. Side- and end-scrapers
   c. Perforators with diamond-shaped cross-section
2. Pecked, ground, and polished stone objects
   a. Spuds
   b. Celts with single bit, tapered poll
   c. Stone "saws"
3. Bone and antler objects
   a. Bone awls, both splinter and deer ulna awls
   b. Bone "harpoon" points
   c. Bone beamers
   d. Worked bear toes
   e. "Mesh spreaders" of turtle plastron

        f. Antler flakers

        g. Antler projectile points or socketted handles

    4. Shell objects

        a. Hemispherical beads of anculosa shell

    5. Metal objects

        a. Wedges or celts of copper

        b. Copper awls

    6. Pottery

        a. Grit-tempered vessels showing both paddle-and-anvil and coiling technique

        b. Paste has granular texture

        c. Cord-roughened or smoothed-over cord-roughened surface treatment

        d. Decoration confined to rim or shoulder

            (1) Imprinting with single cord on interior as well as exterior rim

            (2) Puncturing

            (3) Punctating

            (4) Embossing

            (5) Indentation

            (6) Incising

        e. Vessel form, wide shoulder, open mouth, conoidal base

        f. Pipes, pottery, no temper, simple decoration, elbow type

III. Ceremonial Life

  A. Burial customs

      1. In mounds

        a. Conical

        b. Linear

        c. Effigy

      2. Location

        a. Sub-floor pit

        b. On mound floor

        c. In mound fill

      3. Type of burial

        a. Flesh, flexed

            (1) Single

            (2) Multiple

        b. Bundle reburial

            (1) Single

            (2) Multiple

        c. Combination of a and b

        d. Cremation

            (1) Partial, of either a, b, or c

      4. Mortuary furniture

        a. Rare, no special artifacts

        b. Altars

Chapter IV

AFFILIATIVE ASPECTS OF THE EFFIGY MOUND CULTURE

The principal method of determining cultural relationships among various archaeologically known groups is by means of typology. Typology, as it is used here, is defined as a method of comparing standardized or idealized types with actual artifacts, the basic intent being to extend the spatial and temporal aspects of an assemblage. In other words, objects which appear similar or made by the use of similar techniques and of the same kind of material, are considered either to have stemmed from the same root or have been subject to like influences from an outside source. One of the questions which continues to arise has to do with the problem of whether Effigy Mound is unique in itself or whether it is compounded from the influence of other outside cultural manifestations. McKern (1942, p. 164) says:

"The Effigy Mound Aspect did not come into the state as such; it was entirely a local development, a true product of Wisconsin. There is some evidence that the culture began to assume specific character in northwestern Wisconsin, where the peculiarities of many small mounds and their contents, apparently erected during an early period, are significantly prophetic of Effigy Mound characteristics. This period of formative growth and expansion must have required a considerable passage of time, and there are indications that this interesting Woodland group thrived along the shores of our streams and lakes for a long while, possibly for many centuries."

It is clear that McKern believes Effigy Mound to be native to this province and of considerable antiquity. Griffin (1946, p. 69) apparently sees certain Hopewellian influences in Effigy Mound and assigns it to a Middle Woodland period making it contemporaneous with Hopewellian, for he says, "The allocation to the Effigy Mound Aspect of the copper-bitted implement, the square-sided, copper awls, harpoons, certain pottery traits, and burial customs, some of which also appear in Hopewellian, provokes the suggestion that while Hopewellian in its Ohio and Illinois Valley form was dominating part of the Wisconsin area, much of the state continued its northern Woodland tradition." Bennett (footnote, p. 112) also sees Hopewellian similarities in Effigy Mound and cites his reasons in the statement, "Moreover, a few generalized burial concepts of Hopewellian and Effigy Mound seem close: mound stratification, prepared mound floors, the sub-floor pits with ledges . . . cremation of secondary burials. . . . These traits are rather infrequent in Effigy Mound Aspect also suggest affinity [sic] : copper awls and celts, for example." Martin, Quimby, and Collier (pp. 303-5) also agree to the contemporaniety of Effigy Mound and Hopewellian since they assign Effigy Mound to a period of 700-1300 A.D. and Hopewellian to 900-1300 A.D. They have made no statement, however, regarding the possibility of Hopewellian influence in the earlier developed culture.

TABLE 12

COMPARISON OF WISCONSIN HOPEWELL WITH EFFIGY MOUND*

Material Traits	Trempealeau	Effigy Mound
Conical mounds	Abundant	Abundant
Effigy and linear mounds	. . . .	Abundant
Multiple flesh burials	Abundant	Rare
Bundle reburials	Abundant	Abundant
Burial extended, flesh	Abundant	. . . .
Burials flexed, flesh	. . . .	Abundant
Sub-floor pit burials, in mounds	Abundant	Abundant
Floor burials, in mounds	Abundant	Abundant
Supra-floor burials, in mounds	. . . .	Abundant
Rectilinear burial pits	Abundant	Rare
Curvilinear burial pits	. . . .	Abundant
Grave goods present	Abundant	Rare
Woven fabrics	Present	. . . .
Rouletted pottery	Abundant	Rare
Cord-imprinted pottery	Rare	Abundant
Broad, flat copper axes	Present	Different
Large, chipped-stone knives	Present	. . . .
Obsidian implements	Present	. . . .
Stone platform pipes	Present	. . . .
Pottery pipes	. . . .	Present
Pearl beads	Present	. . . .
Tubular copper beads	Abundant	. . . .
Bear canine ornaments	Present	. . . .
Copper ear-spools	Present	. . . .
Copper plaques	Present	. . . .
Use of silver	Present	. . . .
Polished stone ornaments	Present	. . . .
Copper cone pendants	Present	. . . .
Cradle board deformation of skulls	Present	. . . .

*Modication of table in McKern, *Wisconsin Variant of the Hopewell Culture,* Milwaukee Public Museum Bull. 10, No. 2, 1931, p. 233.

Comparison of the traits of Effigy Mound with those of Wisconsin Hopewell show that certain traits are held in common, as the preceding table indicates.

It is apparent that the similarity between the two cultures lies in the type of mound and type and location of burials within the mounds. However, even with regard to these points the similarity is not complete since only the conical and large oval type mounds occur in Hopewell, while the linear and effigy types accompany the conicals in Effigy Mound. The great Serpent Mound of Ohio is the best known effigy mound to be found in the Hopewellian culture and this is considerably larger than any Wisconsin mound as well as representing a form which is not found in the largest area of Effigy Mound distribution. The Snyder Mound, figured by Bennett (Fig. 19, p. 64) in Jo Davies County, Illinois, shows some resemblance although it is a structure of much smaller size. Other structures of effigy nature which have been identified as Hopewellian include the eagle effigy mound by Magrath (pp. 40-46) in the North Benton Mound, and the eagle-effigy stone mounds in Georgia mentioned by Waring (pp. 119-20) in Facts and Comments, American Antiquity. However, the eagle effigy was a stone-outline figure found *in* a conical mound and not a mound itself. The stone effigies of Georgia apparently are mounds built of stone. Up to the present time, no stone mound effigies have been reported from the Wisconsin Effigy Mound province; such structures are entirely foreign to the culture. Stone- and sometimes bone-outline effigies occur in association with tipi sites in South Dakota (Thomas, 1890, p. 534), but here again the only resemblance of these structures to those of Effigy Mound lies in the animal subjects. An additional breakdown of the burial traits of these cultures follows in Table 13.

TABLE 13

COMPARATIVE BURIAL TRAITS OF WISCONSIN HOPEWELL AND EFFIGY MOUND
(McKern, 1931, p. 237)

Burial Traits	Hopewell	Effigy Mound
Bark associated with burials	Present	. . . .
Rectilinear area for burials	Present	. . . .
Rectilinear sub-floor pits for burials	Present	. . . .
Bark-covered burial floors	Present	. . . .
Humus cleaned floors for burials	Present	Present
Extended-in-the-flesh burials	Present	. . . .
Bundle reburials	Present	Present
Burial of fine artifacts with the dead	Present	. . . .
Multiple flesh burials	Present	Present

As the above Table indicates, many of the characteristic Hopewellian traits do not occur in Effigy Mound. The extended type of burial is not found in the Effigy Mound culture at all. Moreover, the grave goods placed with the Hopewellian dead are special artifacts; as McKern (1931, p. 230) states, "The inclusions of grave goods often must have represented the choicest objects of their material wealth." Mortuary furniture, when it is found in Effigy Mound graves, is no different than the artifacts of ordinary type.

The copper celts and awls of Effigy Mound may actually represent influence from the Hopewell culture, but, on the other hand, copper objects of these types also occur in the Old Copper complex of Wisconsin (Wittry: Fig. 2, group IV, A-1, p. 12; Fig. 3, group VI, G, p. 13).

Certain pottery traits should also be mentioned since they occur in both of these cultures. Vessel shape and use of cord marking are shared by Hopewell and Effigy Mound as well as such decorative techniques as embossed nodes at the rim, punctation, and rocked-dentate stamping. Conoidal-based vessels with an open mouth and constricted neck are common in all Woodland cultures, however, as is the practice of cord marking.

Thus, cultural affiliation between Hopewellian and Effigy Mound in Wisconsin can be reduced to general traits such as burial of the dead in mounds, possible similarity in two types of copper artifacts, and certain generalized or widespread pottery traits including vessel shape and certain methods of decoration. When it is added that the long list of material objects usually associated with Hopewellian has no counterpart in Effigy Mound, the apparent similarity is not so well defined. There is, in addition, a general correspondence between Effigy Mound and other manifestations such as Central Basin and Red Ochre in Illinois, and Mille Lacs in Minnesota. Table 14 lists the Central Basin traits (Cole and Deuel, p. 90) in comparison with those of Effigy Mound.

TABLE 14

COMPARISON OF EFFIGY MOUND AND CENTRAL BASIN TRAITS

Material Traits	Central Basin	Effigy Mound
Low Mound containing burials	Present	Present
Flexed Skeletons	Present	Present
Bundled skeletal remains	Present	Present
Multiple burials	Present	Present
Dog burials	Present	Rare
Shallow piles or layers of stone	Present	Present
Artificial deformation of skull, cradle-board flattening	Present	. . . .

The above are burial mound traits. Traits from the village component of Central Basin also show affinity to Effigy Mound. The stemmed and notched projectile points, scrapers, pottery vessels with a constricted neck and conoidal base exhibiting such decorative techniques as incising, punctating, notching of the lip, et cetera, are all in keeping with the Effigy Mound tradition.

Table 15 compares the traits of Red Ochre (Cole and Deuel, pp. 89-90) and Effigy Mound.

TABLE 15

COMPARISON OF RED OCHRE AND EFFIGY MOUND TRAITS

Material Traits	Red Ochre	Effigy Mound
Burials in low-domed mounds	Present	Present
Flexed burials	Present	Present
Cremated remains	Present	Present
Disarticulated or bundle burials	Present	Present
Burials accompanied by caches	Present	. . . .
Burials with few or no artifacts	Present	Present
Powdered hematite sprinkled over burials	Present	. . . .
Burials without red ochre	Present	Present
Stonework with burials predominant over other materials	Present	Present
Copper plaque found with burial	Rare	. . . .
Metallic hematite, showing facets as if ground for paint	Present	. . . .
Shallow "crematory" basin in mound	Present	Rare
Lanceolate projectile points	Present	Rare
Necklaces of shell beads	Present	Rare
Necklaces of copper beads	Present	. . . .
Crinoid stem discs	Present	. . . .
Gorgets of cut shell	Present	. . . .

The material from the Mille Lacs Aspect is tabulated in Table 16.

Incidentally, it is unfortunate that the material on the Clam River Focus, excavated by a Milwaukee Public Museum field party, has not been published. It may well show some interesting relationships with Mille Lacs.

The manifestations called Central Basin, Red Ochre, and Mille Lacs have not been rigidly defined as yet and it may be that future excavation will add many traits which are not found in Effigy Mound. However, considering the data at hand it is apparent that certain correspondences are to be found among these four cultures. The primary similarities lie in the burial customs and in the pottery types. The latter is a more flexible trait and in general has been given weight by archaeologists in determining cultural relationships. As was pointed out in the discussion of the Hopewellian material, the effigy forms are not found outside of the Effigy Mound culture. The parallelisms which do occur are those that might be expected in comparing any cultures stemming from the Woodland pattern. Certain outside influences can be noted among the Central Basin, Red Ochre, Mille Lacs, and Effigy Mound cultures and these quite likely are Hopewellian. However, Hopewellian influences are less distinct in the Wisconsin Effigy Mound sites than in those of Illinois. Embossed nodes, punctation, and

TABLE 16
COMPARISON OF MILLE LACS AND EFFIGY MOUND TRAITS
(Wilford, 1941, pp. 231-49)

Material Traits	Mille Lacs	Effigy Mound
Burials in low-domed mounds	Present	Present
Bundle reburials	Present	Present
Flesh burials	Present	Present
Cremation	Present	Present
Multiple burials	Present	Present
Grave goods rare	Present	Present
Burials located in :		
a. pits	Present	Present
b. mound floor	Present	Present
c. mound fill	Present	Present
Shouldered pottery vessels with		
constricted neck and conoidal bases	Present	Present
Pottery decorative techniques :		
a. cord-wrapped stick	Present	. . . .
b. cord-wrapped paddle	Present	Present
c. embossed nodes	Present	Present
d. incising	Present	Present
e. cross-hatched rim	Present	. . . .
f. dentate stamping	Present	Rare
Decoration confined to rim area	Present	Present
Stemmed projectile points	Present	Present
Triangular projectile points	Present	. . . .
Copper fish gorges	Present	. . . .
Bone bracelets	Present	. . . .
Elbow pipes	Present	Present
Platform pipes	Present	. . . .

the use of rocked-dentate stamping may mean Hopewellian influence, but certainly not to any great extent. It is very possible that resemblances could be noted also between the traits of Effigy Mound and other burial mound cultures such as Adena and Hamilton. Yet neither of these is found in the Wisconsin province.

Chronological Implications

What can be said concerning the relative chronological position of Effigy Mound? In the first place, the large number of mounds found in a limited area of distribution would seem to indicate a long period of occupation. The fact that the skeletal material is so fragmentary and poorly preserved may point to considerable antiquity. Such factors as acidity of the soil vary from locality to locality and may be partly responsible for rapid deterioration of bone. However, this poor preservation of the bones in Effigy Mound culture is a widespread condition in the state and, therefore, seems to suggest great antiquity. The possible Hopewellian influence, however slight, may also help to establish an earlier date for Effigy Mound. In a recent article, Linton (p. 317) states, ". . . Hopewell, . . . is now dated at about the beginning of the Christian era." This statement is based upon the recent technique of dating by means of radioactive carbon, and although the process itself may be in the experimental stage, revealing results have been obtained.

The only Carbon 14 dates for Effigy Mound come from two mounds in the Effigy Mound National Monument in Iowa (Griffin, 1952, p. 367). One of the mounds, a conical which suggests Illinois Hopewell, yielded a date of 900 plus or minus 300; and a bear effigy which was dated at 930 plus or minus 300. The author suggests that these dates probably lie nearer to the end dates for Effigy Mound than the beginning of the culture.

A panther mound (Mound 26) reported by Maxwell from the Diamond Bluff Site* provides some interesting data on the time span of Effigy Mound. Maxwell (p. 442) summarizes the data as follows:

"This then is the basic data derived from Mound 26: (1) The panther-shaped mound itself which is considered to be an early trait in the Woodland complex. (2) The sub-mound pit containing a flexed burial, also Woodland traits. (3) One arrowhead which is Woodland in character and one which is more similar to the Mississippian complex. (4) The small, loop-handled bowl which is characteristic of the Orr Focus—Oneota Aspect, Mississippi Phase. (5) A fragment of a clay bowl, found on the edge of the sub-mound pit, which is Middle Mississippi in character. (6) A burial which was made during the construction period of the mound, and with which is associated a bowl in which are combined style elements of both Upper and Middle Mississippi culture. (7) The suggestion that the old woman and the child in the pit and the twelve year old boy placed in the mound fill belonged to the same family, since all three had abnormally large teeth.

"An interpretation of these apparently conflicting facts can be made only after a reanalysis of our existing frame of reference. First, since there is no reason to doubt that the effigy mound complex is early in Wisconsin, we must assume either that the idea of the animal-shaped burial mound persisted until late times in some areas, or that Upper Mississippi culture begins in Wisconsin much earlier than we had previously supposed. In all probability the true picture is a compromise between the two suggestions."

The suggestion is made that Effigy Mound began at a relatively early time and continued to exist in parts, if not in all, of its known area until the time of the introduction of the Mississippi culture.

---

* The Diamond Bluff Site is probably related to the Grand River culture. See Jeske, *The Grand River Mound Group and Campsite.* Milwaukee Public Museum Bull. 3, No. 2, 1927.

Although it is tentative, there is some evidence for speaking of a proto-Effigy Mound period. In Burnett county, northwest Wisconsin, a few conical and linear mounds have been opened which contained no burials. The sub-floor pits as well as the usual associated altars were present. In fact, the material contained within them is the same as that of the effigy forms. However, no effigies were included in the group. The supposition is that the mounds are so old that all trace of the bones has disappeared. This implies that the earliest manifestation of the Effigy Mound culture was limited to conical and linear forms and that the effigy mounds came in somewhat later.

Identification With Historic Groups

Various attempts have been made to assign the Effigy Mound culture to a specific historically known Indian group. One of these, the theory of Thomas, simply attributed the mounds to the Siouan tribes. Thomas (1890, pp. 709-10) says :

". . . there are some good reasons for believing that the effigy mounds and those works belonging to the same system are attributable to one or more tribes of the Siouan stock. As has been shown in the preceding part of the volume, the custom of placing the small tumuli in lines connected and disconnected to form the wall-like mounds seems to have been peculiar to the builders of the effigies. Following up this hint and tracing the transitions in form from what appears to be the more ancient to the more recent types, we are led to the comparatively modern surface figures of the Siouan tribes."

Thomas quotes Morgan and Lubbock rather extensively in this regard and apparently derives the transition from the effigy mound to the Siouan stone or bone outline figures through reasoning of the classical evolutionary type. This type of reasoning is speculation rather than history and does not hold. Archaeologically, there is no evidence to show that the effigies are the forerunners of the Siouan stone outline figures.

The most popular tribes selected as the builders of effigy mounds have been the Winnebago and the Menomini. Radin (1911, p. 517; 1915, pp. 76-103) has argued that the effigy mounds are the work of the Winnebago, but McKern (1928, pp. 277-279) has succeeded in pointing out such flaws in Radin's theory that it cannot be accepted as valid. One of the possible explanations of the forms of effigy mounds is that they represent the totem or clan symbols of various groups. We cannot determine this archaeologically, nor can we, even should we accept such an explanation, determine whether the type of totemism is similar to that of the Australian aborigines or the Iroquois. The fact remains, however, that the effigy mounds provide evidence of a man-nature relationship. In order to test the idea of clan and mound identity we must first discover the tribes which inhabited the region in historic times. These are listed below along with the clan names which have been identified in each tribe.

MENOMINI

I *Bear phratry*
   Clans: Bear, Mud-turtle, Porcupine, Beaver, Muskrat
II *Eagle phratry*
   Clans: Bald-eagle, Crow, Raven, Red-tail Hawk, Golden Eagle,
      Fish-hawk
III *Crane phratry*
   Clans: Crane, Great Heron, Old Squaw, Duck, Coot
IV *Wolf phratry*
   Clans: Wolf, Dog, Deer
 V *Moose phratry*
   Clans: Moose, Elk, Marten, Fisher

CHIPPEWA

Clans: Catfish, Merman, Lynx, Moose, Goose, Whitefish, Gull, Wolf,
Bear, Beaver, Mud-turtle, Snapping Turtle, Little Turtle, Reindeer, Snipe,
Crane, Pigeon-hawk (Raven), Bald Eagle, Loon, Duck (Swan), Duck,
Snake, Muskrat, Marten, Heron, Bullhead, Sturgeon, Pike, Pickerel, Forked
Tree.

CHIWERE SIOUX

(Oto, Missouri and Iowa)

Clans: Wolf, Bear, Cow Buffalo, Elk, Eagle, Pigeon, Snake, Owl,
Beaver, Black Bear, (Thunder, Red Earth are extinct).

FOX

Clans: Bear, Fox Wolf, Elk, Big Lynx, Buffalo, Swan, Pheasant, Eagle,
Sea, Sturgeon, Bass, Thunder, Bear, Potato, Raccoon, Beaver, Otter, Deer,
Hawk, Fish, Bone, Big Tree, Ringed Perch, Water.

SAUK

Clans: Trout, Sturgeon, Bass, Great Lynx, Sea Fox, Wolf, Bear, Indian
Potato, Elk, Swan, Grouse, Eagle, Thunder, Buffalo, Fish, Beaver, Deer,
Turkey.

WINNEBAGO

Clans: Thunderbird, War People, Eagle, Pigeon, Bear, Wolf, Water
Spirit, Deer, Elk, Buffalo, Fish, Snake.

MASCOUTEN

(Prairie Potawatomi, not 17th century Mascouten)

Clans: Fish, Great Sea, Thunderbird, Bald Eagle, Black Eagle, Duck-
hawk, Raven, Sea Gull, Loon, Turkey, Buffalo, Moose, Elk, Deer, Bear,
Grizzly Bear, White Rabbit, Wolf, Dog, Fox, Raccoon.

There is a certain amount of overlapping in the clan names of the various groups listed above. However, inspection shows that there are seventy-one distinct names included. These are:

Wolf	Ringed Perch	Berry	Goose
Pigeon	Deer	Crow	Pike
Thunder	Great Sea	Crane	Eagle
Pheasant	Sea Gull	Marten	Black Bear
Big Tree	Raccoon	Reindeer	Big Lynx
Grouse	Muskrat	Snipe	Bone
Water Spirit	Fish-hawk	Elk	Indian Potato
Duck-hawk	Catfish	Beaver	Thunderbird
White Rabbit	Whitefish	Swan	Black Eagle
Porcupine	Bullhead	Bass	Grizzly Bear
Golden Eagle	Buffalo	Trout	Mud-turtle
Old Squaw	Owl	Turkey	Red-tail Hawk
Merman	Fox	Raven	Great Heron
Little Turtle	Sturgeon	Moose	Fisher
Bear	Water	Dog	Snapping Turtle
Snake	War People	Man	Pickerel
Red Earth	Bald Eagle	Duck	Forked Tree
Sea	Loon	Coot	

As was mentioned before, the forms of the effigy mounds cannot be positively identified as representing certain specific animal or bird forms. The thirteen mound types set forth earlier are based on the many varied terms which have been applied to the mounds, and several terms were combined under a single heading; for example, duck, eagle, et cetera, were simply called bird mounds. The same method must be used with regard to the clan names in order to make the data comparable. One way of combining the names is as follows:

BIRD

Eagle, Pigeon, Owl, Swan, Pheasant, Grouse, Turkey, Bald Eagle, Black Eagle, Golden Eagle, Duck-hawk, Raven, Sea Gull, Loon, Crow, Red-tail Hawk, Fish Hawk, Crane, Great Heron, Duck, Coot, Fisher, Goose, Snipe, Thunderbird, Man (?), Merman (?).

FISH

Sturgeon, Bass, Ringed Perch, Trout, Catfish, Whitefish, Bullhead, Pike, Pickerel.

CANINE

Wolf, Fox, Dog, Marten.

DEER

Deer, Elk, Moose, White Rabbit (?), Reindeer.

BEAVER

Beaver, Raccoon, Porcupine, Muskrat, Otter.

TURTLE

Mud-turtle, Snapping Turtle, Little Turtle.

BUFFALO

Buffalo, Cow Buffalo.

PANTHER

SNAKE

ABSTRACT IDEAS

Thunder, Red Earth, Sea, Bone, Tree, Water, Indian Potato, War People, Water Spirit, Berry.

It is obvious that the above groupings are based on similarity of form rather than upon a zoological or genetic classification. The combinations attempted here simply represent one of the several possible ways in which it might be done. The category of Abstract Ideas might be different, since it could be argued that the name Berry can be identified with the conical form, Bone as biconical, Indian Potato as oval, et cetera. It is also realized that this arrangement is arbitrary in the same way that the establishment of mound types is arbitrary. Table 17, on the following page, should be examined with these things in mind. The correlations found in Table 17 are to be considered as exceedingly general. It is impossible to break down the mound types in as much detail as it is with the clan names. That is, we can speak of the Duck, Hawk, Eagle, and Owl clans, but we cannot positively identify the bird effigies as such. Therefore, all of the clan names that are those of birds are simply lumped into a bird category for the purposes of comparison. The large category of non-comparable clan names, including forms foreign to the Effigy Mound culture as well as those names which have to do with abstract ideas such as Water Spirit, Red Earth, and Thunder, has no counterpart in Effigy Mound even if we include the problematical forms. In addition, such correlation as does exist is weakened by the fact that at least half of the mounds of the Effigy Mound culture are conical, and a large number are linear or oval. These forms do not tie up with the clan names of the tribes.

TABLE 17

CORRELATION OF CLAN NAMES WITH EFFIGY MOUND TYPES

Names of clans and types of Mounds	Effigy Mound	Tribes							
		Menomini	Chippewa	Chiwere	Fox	Sauk	Winnebago	Mascouten	Kickapoo
Panther	34	0	1	0	1	1	0	0	0
Bear	20	1	1	1	1	1	1	2	1
Bird	24	11	10	3	3	3	3	8	3
Deer	11	2	2	1	2	2	2	4	1
Buffalo	1	0	0	1	1	1	1	1	0
Turtle	4	1	4	0	0	0	0	0	0
Canine	16	4	2	1	2	2	1	3	2
Beaver	1	3	2	1	3	1	0	1	0
Non-comparable clan names: fish, snake and abstract ideas		1	9	3	10	7	4	2	4

This Table does not indicate which of the known historic tribes was responsible for the Effigy Mound culture, but does eliminate at least two of the tribes. The Kickapoo possess only four out of eight clan names which are comparable to the effigy mound forms, and have four clan names which do not have effigy counterparts. The Winnebago have five out of eight clan names which correspond to mound types and also have four clan names which do not compare with the mound forms. The Menomini, Chiwere, and Mascouten have six out of eight clan names in common with the mound types and, in addition, have few names which do not correspond to the mound forms. The Chippewa, Sauk, and Fox have seven out of eight clan names which can be correlated with the mound types but each has a large number of names which cannot be related to the effigy mounds. We cannot conclude that the mounds were the work of one of the latter tribes because of the previously stated weaknesses in the comparison.

The tribes listed in the Table are known to have been in the Wisconsin province during historic times, but some of them may not have inhabited the region in the prehistoric period. It must also be considered that there may have been tribes in the area during prehistoric times that left before the coming of the whites. We can only conclude, then, that neither the Kickapoo nor the Winnebago were responsible for the Effigy Mound culture. In fact, none of the historic Woodland clan systems tie in very well with the effigy mound shapes, nor have any of these groups built mounds of this type during the historic period. With regard to the Blackfoot, Assiniboin, and other tribes of the Plains region and elsewhere that may have come from this region at one time, the data are uncertain and imperfectly known. Attempts at correlation of their social systems and the Effigy Mound types are even more fruitless. Consequently, the clan theory of the mound purpose can be discarded.

Chapter V

CONCLUSIONS AND SPECULATIONS

The people who conceived and carried on the way of life which is known archaeologically as the Effigy Mound culture, have left behind few remains from which their story can be written. The culture as a whole is only imperfectly understood, the primary data relating to what is presumably a small portion of the ceremonial life, the burial customs. However, excavation has provided sufficient data to warrant drawing it together at this time before much more extensive work is carried on.

We know from the numerous, but poorly preserved skeletal material only that the people themselves were longheaded and that they did not practice cradleboard deformation.

The Effigy Mound culture appears to have been an indigenous development in the Wisconsin province, one which grew up out of a basic Woodland origin with little discernible outside influence. Bennett's (p. 111) statement that some of the distinctive traits for the Jo Daviess Focus are those which may reflect an influence from Hopewellian manifestations holds true for the northern Illinois mounds, but many of the recurrent traits of the mounds of this area are foreign to those of the Wisconsin province. In general, we can consider the mounds of Minnesota, Iowa, and Illinois to be marginal to Effigy Mound culture as it is defined in the region of its greatest prevalence. Consideration of Wisconsin as the center of Effigy Mound development and the surrounding areas as marginal is not comparable to saying that Ohio is the center of Hopewellian development and that all other areas are peripheral, because the distribution of Effigy Mound is exceedingly confined and limited, whereas Hopewellian manifestations are far flung. In fact, the limited distribution of Effigy Mound is an argument in favor of its distinctiveness as a culture as well as its indigenous development in the area which it occupies.

The meagre midden deposits in the campsites near the mound groups and the lack of permanent villages which can be identified as Effigy Mound has led to the assumption that the people were semi-nomadic hunters and food gatherers. The idea has been advanced that the presence of pottery in any culture is evidence for that group having knowledge of and actually practicing agriculture (Setzler, p. 254). Should this be the case the Effigy Mound people would have to be considered more or less permanent agriculturalists, in view of the fact that pottery is found in association with the mounds. However, the concept of the "Agpo Base" remains inferential. The content of the list of material traits of Effigy Mound also bears out the supposition that these people lived a semi-nomadic type of life.

The burial customs which can be determined archaeologically indicate that the Effigy Mound builders buried their dead in low mounds shaped in conical, linear, and effigy forms. The latter is one of the most distinctive traits of the entire assemblage. The idea has been advanced that only important persons were buried in the effigies. This is questionable since we find not only male skeletons, which might conceivably be the remains of chiefs or other dignitaries, but also the skeletal remains of women and children who are not so likely to have been of great importance.

In addition, we do not find effigy mound cemeteries. Some of the mounds do not appear to have contained burials, but it may be that the bones in these mounds have so completely decomposed that all evidence of their previous existence is gone except for indication through discoloration of the soil.

Some of the problems surrounding the Effigy Mound culture involve the purpose of the mounds. Why were they built and why do they assume such varied shapes? If they are burial mounds, why is it that we find a wide variety of burial types? Although it is highly speculative, the writer would like to advance the following hypothesis: It is possible that the mounds of the Effigy Mound culture represent symbols, in many cases unidentifiable, having to do with certain ceremonial practices, perhaps some religious rite involving animals. This does not necessarily imply totemism, since the whole range of totems is not involved. But for whatever reason, the mounds were probably built at specific times, say once a year, undoubtedly during the spring or summer when the ground is thawed and soft. At the time of mound construction, all persons who had died during the preceding period were buried in the mounds. This would account for the fact that we find both single and multiple burials. Those who died nearest to the time of mound building would be buried in the flesh, whereas the bundle reburials would represent the persons who had died during the winter and had been set up on scaffolds because the ground was frozen, making digging impractical. The large multiple bundle reburials of thirty-five or more individuals might be the remains of those who were killed in a battle or who died as the result of an epidemic or of starvation. An alternate possibility is that the large multiple bundle reburials might represent a periodic burial ceremony in which individuals previously disposed of were gathered for multiple interment. The single family units of each small group may have been responsible for burying their own dead, respectively, and more than one mound may have been built at one time.

The mounds seldom occur more than fifty to a given group and often include fewer than that. This might be explained by the fact that the Effigy Mound people were hunters and gatherers. There is abundant evidence to show that the hunting and gathering peoples of the present day must live in small groups and move periodically in search of food in the form of game which has been scattered as a result of the proximity of human habitation, and of wild roots and plants which have become scarce in a picked-over area. The same thing may have been true of the Effigy Mound builders. Such small, wandering groups might have returned from year to year to the same spot to build their ceremonial tumuli until the time when the food quest had taken them so far from the mound group that the trip through a temporarily foodless area would be inadvisable. They would then begin another group in a new location and return to it until again forced to move to another place for lack of food. Hostile Indians or scarcity of food may have caused them to abandon a site before many mounds had been constructed, which would account for the Utley Group with only seven mounds, and the Green Lake Site with only one. There is also the possibility that other groups of Effigy Mound people, in their wanderings, came upon mound groups that had been left by a previous band and, sufficient time having elapsed for the repopulation of game animals and food plants, they then added their particular types of mounds to those already built. This could account for the diversity of mound forms in a given group.

An alternate hypothesis might be a possible tie-up between the mound forms and the guardian spirit concept. This concept was widespread in this area and usually involved animal and bird forms.

As was stated earlier, these ideas are merely speculative. However, they do take into account the major traits and, therefore, fit the facts as we know them to a large degree.

Attempts to relate Effigy Mound customs to those of known historic cultures have been constructive in terms of the Woodland cultures. Such items as "mesh spreaders," scaffold burials, use of the bow and arrow, scattered community life, bone beamers, the importance of ceremonial smoking, and the general economy all have their counterparts in modern-day groups. Most of the tribes came into the area in relatively recent times and it is not certain which of them lived here before the contact period. The only Woodland groups in the area before the advent of the white man seem to have been the Menomini and the Winnebago. It is certain that none of the groups built mounds typical of the Effigy Mound culture after the coming of the whites. Just as we can show a general connection archaeologically with cultures stemming from a Woodland origin, so can we demonstrate only a general similarity between Effigy Mound and the historic Woodland groups of the present day.

It can be stated with reasonable certainty that the Effigy Mound culture itself has considerable antiquity. The earlier manifestations, at least, seem to equate in time with early Wisconsin Woodland and Hopewell, the oldest mound-building culture in the state (McKern, 1931, p. 241).

Appendixes

APPENDIX A

CHART 1
DISTRIBUTION OF BURIALS BY TYPES

Conical Mounds

Site	Md. No.	Single Flesh	Single Reburial	Crema-tion	Multiple Flesh	Multiple Reburial	Indeter.
Neale	64	1					
McClaughry I	3					1	1
	4					1	
	5					1	
	6		1				
	9			1			
	11		1				
	15		2				
	19		1				
	23		1				
	25	1					
	37	1					
	38		1				1
	39						
	40	1	1				
	41					1	
	45					1	
	46					1	
	47	1					
	53	1	1				
	59						1
McClaughry II	12						1
	14						1
	18						1
	21						1
	34	1					
Nitschke	3	1					1
	4		2				
	15		1				
	16						1
	17	1				1	
	18		1				
	43		1				1
	51						1
	54	1					
Kratz Creek	1					1	
	8			1			
	50						1

(Table Continued on Next Page)

Site	Md. No.	Single		Crema-tion	Multiple		Indeter.
		Flesh	Reburial		Flesh	Reburial	
Raisbeck	1					1	
	2				1		
	3					1	
	4	1					
	8				1		
	24					1	
	40					1	
	64					1	
	65					1	
	66					1	

Oval Mounds

Site	Md. No.	Single		Crema-tion	Multiple		Indeter.
		Flesh	Reburial		Flesh	Reburial	
Green Lake	1	1					
McClaughry I	28		2		2	1	
	51		1			1	
Kletzien	19	1					
	25						1
Nitschke	44				1		

Biconical Mounds

Site	Md. No.	Single		Crema-tion	Multiple		Indeter.
		Flesh	Reburial		Flesh	Reburial	
McClaughry I	8	1	2				1
	24		1				

Linear Mounds

Site	Md. No.	Single		Crema-tion	Multiple		Indeter.
		Flesh	Reburial		Flesh	Reburial	
Kletzien	8		1				
	33	3					
	49	1					
Raisbeck	7						1
	18	1					

Bird Mounds

Site	Md. No.	Single Flesh	Single Reburial	Crema-tion	Multiple Flesh	Multiple Reburial	Indeter.
Neale	4						1
	6	1	1				
McClaughry I	55		1				
	40	1					
	56						1
Raisbeck	10			•			1
	23	1					
	31					1	

Panther Mounds

Site	Md. No.	Single Flesh	Single Reburial	Crema-tion	Multiple Flesh	Multiple Reburial	Indeter.
Utley	3	1					
Neale	2						2
	7	1					
McClaughry I	32	2					
Kletzien	2	2					
	3		1				
Nitschke	14	1					
	21		1				
	36	1					
	39	1					
Kratz Creek	3	1	2				
	40						1
	41	1					
Diamond Bluff	26	1			1		
Heller	1	1					

Bear Mounds

Site	Md. No.	Single Flesh	Single Reburial	Crema-tion	Multiple Flesh	Multiple Reburial	Indeter.
Neale	5						1
	10						1
	11	1					
	19					1	

Deer Mounds

| Site | Md. No. | Single | | Crema-tion | Multiple | | Indeter. |
		Flesh	Reburial		Flesh	Reburial	
Kletzien	6	1		1			
	10	1					
	27	1	1				
Nitschke	42						1
Kratz Creek	9			2			

Buffalo Mounds

| Site | Md. No. | Single | | Crema-tion | Multiple | | Indeter. |
		Flesh	Reburial		Flesh	Reburial	
Nitschke	9	1	1				

Turtle Mounds

| Site | Md. No. | Single | | Crema-tion | Multiple | | Indeter. |
		Flesh	Reburial		Flesh	Reburial	
Nitschke	10					2	
	50						2

Beaver Mounds

| Site | Md. No. | Single | | Crema-tion | Multiple | | Indeter. |
		Flesh	Reburial		Flesh	Reburial	
Neale	1	1					

Canine Mounds

| Site | Md. No. | Single | | Crema-tion | Multiple | | Indeter. |
		Flesh	Reburial		Flesh	Reburial	
Raisbeck	11						2

Problematical Mounds

Site	Md. No.	Single		Crema-tion	Multiple		Indeter.
		Flesh	Reburial		Flesh	Reburial	
Neale	47						1
McClaughry I	13						3
	49	1	2			1	
	57	1				1	
Kletzien	4						1
	9						1
	18						1
	24						1
Nitschke	20					1	1
	31	1					
	37	1					
	45	1					
	52	1					

CHART 2

DISTRIBUTION OF TOTAL FEATURES IN MOUNDS

Type of Mound	Altar	Cist	Pit	Misc.
Conical	41	20	1	2
Oval	1	2	0	0
Biconical	3	0	0	0
Linear	1	0	2	0
Panther	6	0	0	0
Bear	12	2	0	0
Bird	2	0	0	0
Deer	2	0	0	0
Buffalo	1	0	0	0
Turtle	1	0	0	0
Canine	0	0	0	0
Beaver	0	0	0	0
Problematical	14	2	0	0

CHART 3

DISTRIBUTION OF SINGLE FEATURES IN MOUNDS

Type of Mound	Altar	Cist	Pit	Misc.
Conical	10	3	0	2
Oval	1	0	0	0
Biconical	1	0	1	0
Linear	1	0	0	0
Panther	4	0	0	0
Bear	2	0	0	0
Bird	2	0	0	0
Deer	2	0	0	0
Buffalo	1	0	0	0
Turtle	1	0	0	0
Canine	0	0	0	0
Beaver	0	0	0	0
Problematical	6	1	0	0

CHART 4

DISTRIBUTION OF MULTIPLE FEATURES IN MOUNDS

Conical Mounds

Site	Mound Number	Altar	Cist	Pit	Misc.
Neale	39	0	2	0	0
	40	0	3	0	0
	41	0	3	0	0
	42	2	2	0	0
	50	2	1	0	0
McClaughry	4	1	0	1	0
	5	0	2	0	0
	25	2	0	0	0
	45	1	2	0	0
	47	0	2	0	0
Kratz Creek	1	10	0	0	0
Raisbeck	1	4	0	0	0
	3	2	0	0	0
	4	4	0	0	0
	39	1	0	0	0
	65	2	0	0	0

Bear Mounds

Site	Mound Number	Altar	Cist	Pit	Misc.
Neale	11	2	0	0	0
	19	2	2	0	0
McClaughry	52	3	0	0	0
Kratz Creek	4	3	0	0	0

Problematical Mounds

Site	Mound Number	Altar	Cist	Pit	Misc.
Neale	47	2	1	0	0
McClaughry	13	4	0	0	0
Ross	3	2	0	0	0

Miscellaneous Mounds

Site	Mound Number	Mound Type	Altar	Cist	Pit	Misc.
McClaughry	8	Biconical	2	0	0	0
	32	Panther	2	0	0	0
	51	Oval	0	2	0	0
Ross	23	Linear	0	0	0	2

APPENDIX B

Two of the copper celts or wedges shown in Plate XXI were found at the Trowbridge Mound Group, a site excavated by a Milwaukee Public Museum field party, directed by W. C. McKern, in 1929. The group is located on the east bank of the mouth of the Trempealeau River in Pirot State Park near Mt. Trempealeau, Trempealeau County, Wisconsin. The site was not completely excavated nor has the material been published.

Bibliography

Barrett, S. A.
   1933.   Ancient Aztalan. Milwaukee Public Museum Bull. 13.
Barrett, S. A. and Hawkes, E. W.
   1919.   The Kratz Creek Mound Group. Milwaukee Public Museum Bull.
           3, No. 1.
Barrett, S. A. and Skinner, A.
   1932.   Certain Mounds and Village Sites of Shawano and Oconto Coun-
           ties, Wisconsin. Milwaukee Public Museum Bull. 10, No. 5.
Baerreis, D.
   1953.   Blackhawk Village Site, (Da5) Dane County, Wisconsin. Journal,
           Iowa Archaeological Society, Vol. 2, No. 4. McGregor, Iowa.
Bennett, J. W.
   1945.   Archaeological Explorations in Jo Daviess County, Illinois. Uni-
           versity of Chicago Press.
Braidwood, R. J.
   1946.   The Order of Incompleteness of the Archaeological Record. Human
           Origins, Selected Readings, Series 2 (2nd edit.), University of
           Chicago (mimeographed).
Cole, F. C. and Deuel, T.
   1937.   Rediscovering Illinois. University of Chicago Press.
Cooper, L. R.
   1933.   Red Cedar Variant of the Wisconsin Hopewell Culture. Milwaukee
           Public Museum Bull. 16, No. 2.
Folge, L.
   1915.   Indian Remains in Manitowoc County. Wisconsin Archeologist
           (O.S.), Vol. 14, No. 4. Milwaukee.
Griffin, J. B.
   1946.   Cultural Change and Continuity in Eastern United States Archae-
           ology. Papers of the Robert S. Peabody Foundation for Archaeology,
           Vol. 3. Andover.
Griffin, J. B. (ed.)
   1952.   Archaeology of the Eastern United States. Univ. Chicago Press.
Haven, S. F.
   1856.   Archaeology of the United States. Smithsonian Contributions to
           Knowledge, Vol. 8.
Hodge, F. W.
   1907.   Handbook of American Indians North of Mexico. Bureau of Ameri-
           can Ethnology Bulletin 30, Parts 1 and 2.
Hoffman, W. J.
   1892-3.   The Menominee Indians. Bureau of American Ethnology, 14th
             Ann. Rept.
Jennings, J.
   1948.   A Summary of the Culture of the Effigy Mound Builders. Prepared
           as a guide to research in conjunction with the development of Effigy
           Mound National Park. (Unpublished.)

Jeske, J. A.
    1927.   The Grand River Mound Group and Campsite. Milwaukee Public
            Museum Bull. 3, No. 2.
Jones, W.
    1937.   Ethnography of the Fox. Bureau of American Ethnology Bull. 125.
Keyes, C. R.
    1927.   Prehistoric Man in Iowa. The Palimpsest, Vol. 8, No. 6. Cornell,
            Iowa.
Kinietz, W. V.
    1940.   The Indians of the Western Great Lakes 1615-1760. University of
            Michigan Press.
Lapham, I. A.
    1855.   Antiquities of Wisconsin. Smithsonian Contributions to Knowledge,
            Vol. 7.
Linton, R.
    1951.   New Light on Ancient America. The Scientific Monthly, Vol. 72,
            No. 5. Baltimore.
MacGrath, W. H.
    1945.   The North Benton Mound: A Hopewell Site in Ohio. American
            Antiquity, Vol. 11, No. 1. Menasha, Wis.
Martin, Paul S., Quimby, G. I., and Collier, D.
    1947.   Indians Before Columbus. University of Chicago Press.
Maxwell, M. S.
    1950.   A Change in the Interpretation of Wisconsin's Prehistory. Wis-
            consin Magazine of History, Vol. 33, No. 4. Madison, Wis.
McKern, W. C.
    1928.   The Neale and McClaughry Mound Groups. Milwaukee Public
            Museum Bull. 3, No. 3.
    1930.   The Kletzien and Nitschke Mound Groups. Milwaukee Public Mu-
            seum Bull. 3, No. 4.
    1931.   A Wisconsin Variant of the Hopewell Culture. Milwaukee Public
            Museum Bull. 10, No. 2.
    1942.   First Settlers of Wisconsin. Wisconsin Magazine of History, Vol.
            26, No. 2. Madison.
    1945.   Preliminary Report on the Upper Mississippi Phase in Wisconsin.
            Milwaukeee Public Museum Bull. 16, No. 3.
McKern, W. C. and Ritzenthaler, R. E.
    1949.   Trait List of the Effigy Mound Aspect. Wisconsin Archeologist,
            Vol. 30 (N.S.), No. 2. Milwaukee.
Michelson, T.
    1937.   Fox Miscellany. Bureau of American Ethnology, Bull. 114.
Mott, Mildred
    1938.   The Relation of Historic Indian Tribes to Archaeological Mani-
            festations in Iowa. Iowa Journal of History and Politics, Vol. 36,
            No. 3. Des Moines.

Nash, P.
  1933. The Excavations of Ross Mound Group I. Milwaukee Public Museum Bull. 16, No. 1.
Radin, P.
  1911. Some Aspects of Winnebago Archaeology. American Anthropologist, Vol. 13 (N.S.), No. 4. Menasha, Wis.
  1915-6. The Winnebago Tribe. Bureau of American Ethnology, 37th Ann. Rept.
Setzler, F. M.
  1940. Archaeological Perspectives in the Northern Mississippi Valley. Smithsonian Miscellaneous Collections, Vol. C.
Shetrone, H. C.
  1926. Exploration of the Hopewell Group of Prehistoric Earthworks. Ohio Archaeological and Historical Quarterly, Vol. 35, No. 1. Columbus.
Skinner, A.
  1923. Observations on the Ethnology of the Sauk Indians. Milwaukee Public Museum Bull. 5, No. 1.
  1924. The Mascoutens or Prairie Potawatomi. Milwaukee Public Museum Bull. 6, No. 1.
  1926. Ethnology of the Iowa Indians. Milwaukee Public Museum Bull. 5, No. 4.
Squier, E. G. and Davis, E. H.
  1947. Ancient Monuments of the Mississippi Valley. Smithsonian Contributions to Knowledge, Vol. I.
Taylor, W. W.
  1948. A Study of Archaeology. American Anthropologist, Vol. 50(N.S.), No. 3, Part 2; Memoir No. 69. Menasha, Wis.
Thomas, C.
  1883-4. Burial Mounds of the Northern Section of the United States. Bureau of American Ethnology, 5th Ann. Rept.
  1890-1. Report on the Mound Explorations of the Bureau of Ethnology. Bureau of American Ethnology, 12th Ann. Rept.
Waring, A. J., Jr.
  1945. "Hopewellian" Elements in Northern Georgia. American Antiquity, Vol. 11, No. 2. Menasha, Wis.
Wilford, L. A.
  1941. A Tentative Classification of the Prehistoric Cultures of Minnesota. American Antiquity, Vol. 6, No. 3. Menasha, Wis.
  1944. The Prehistoric Indians of Minnesota: The Mille Lacs Aspect. Minnesota History, Vol. 25, No. 4. Minneapolis.
Wissler, C.
  1941. North American Indians of the Plains. American Museum of Natural History, Handbook No. 1. New York.
Wittry, W. L.
  1951. A Preliminary Study of the Old Copper Complex. Wisconsin Archeologist, Vol. 32(N.S.), No. 1. Milwaukee.

DATE DUE

GAYLORD			PRINTED IN U.S.A.